C-4342   CAREER EXAMINATION SERIES

This is your
PASSBOOK for...

Public Service Clerk

Test Preparation Study Guide
Questions & Answers

COPYRIGHT NOTICE

This book is SOLELY intended for, is sold ONLY to, and its use is RESTRICTED to individual, bona fide applicants or candidates who qualify by virtue of having seriously filed applications for appropriate license, certificate, professional and/or promotional advancement, higher school matriculation, scholarship, or other legitimate requirements of education and/or governmental authorities.

This book is NOT intended for use, class instruction, tutoring, training, duplication, copying, reprinting, excerption, or adaptation, etc., by:

1) Other publishers
2) Proprietors and/or Instructors of "Coaching" and/or Preparatory Courses
3) Personnel and/or Training Divisions of commercial, industrial, and governmental organizations
4) Schools, colleges, or universities and/or their departments and staffs, including teachers and other personnel
5) Testing Agencies or Bureaus
6) Study groups which seek by the purchase of a single volume to copy and/or duplicate and/or adapt this material for use by the group as a whole without having purchased individual volumes for each of the members of the group
7) Et al.

Such persons would be in violation of appropriate Federal and State statutes.

PROVISION OF LICENSING AGREEMENTS – Recognized educational, commercial, industrial, and governmental institutions and organizations, and others legitimately engaged in educational pursuits, including training, testing, and measurement activities, may address request for a licensing agreement to the copyright owners, who will determine whether, and under what conditions, including fees and charges, the materials in this book may be used them. In other words, a licensing facility exists for the legitimate use of the material in this book on other than an individual basis. However, it is asseverated and affirmed here that the material in this book CANNOT be used without the receipt of the express permission of such a licensing agreement from the Publishers. Inquiries re licensing should be addressed to the company, attention rights and permissions department.

All rights reserved, including the right of reproduction in whole or in part, in any form or by any means, electronic or mechanical, including photocopying, recording, or by any information storage and retrieval system, without permission in writing from the Publisher.

Copyright © 2025 by
National Learning Corporation

212 Michael Drive, Syosset, NY 11791
(516) 921-8888 • www.passbooks.com
E-mail: info@passbooks.com

PASSBOOK® SERIES

THE *PASSBOOK® SERIES* has been created to prepare applicants and candidates for the ultimate academic battlefield – the examination room.

At some time in our lives, each and every one of us may be required to take an examination – for validation, matriculation, admission, qualification, registration, certification, or licensure.

Based on the assumption that every applicant or candidate has met the basic formal educational standards, has taken the required number of courses, and read the necessary texts, the *PASSBOOK® SERIES* furnishes the one special preparation which may assure passing with confidence, instead of failing with insecurity. Examination questions – together with answers – are furnished as the basic vehicle for study so that the mysteries of the examination and its compounding difficulties may be eliminated or diminished by a sure method.

This book is meant to help you pass your examination provided that you qualify and are serious in your objective.

The entire field is reviewed through the huge store of content information which is succinctly presented through a provocative and challenging approach – the question-and-answer method.

A climate of success is established by furnishing the correct answers at the end of each test.

You soon learn to recognize types of questions, forms of questions, and patterns of questioning. You may even begin to anticipate expected outcomes.

You perceive that many questions are repeated or adapted so that you can gain acute insights, which may enable you to score many sure points.

You learn how to confront new questions, or types of questions, and to attack them confidently and work out the correct answers.

You note objectives and emphases, and recognize pitfalls and dangers, so that you may make positive educational adjustments.

Moreover, you are kept fully informed in relation to new concepts, methods, practices, and directions in the field.

You discover that you are actually taking the examination all the time: you are preparing for the examination by "taking" an examination, not by reading extraneous and/or supererogatory textbooks.

In short, this PASSBOOK®, used directedly, should be an important factor in helping you to pass your test.

PUBLIC SERVICE CLERK

DUTIES
Under direct supervision, performs a variety of clerical tasks in rendering service to the public in obtaining or retaining driving privileges and in the registration and titling of motor vehicles in the State in a vehicle or driver services facility.

DUTIES AND RESPONSIBILITIES
Serves as information clerk directing applicants and public to proper areas of the facility to receive service. Reviews and completes driver's license applications or motor vehicle registration or title applications for processing while gathering all pertinent information to serve the applicant. Administers vision tests to driver's license applicants; codes applications according to results. Administers and grades written driver examinations; explains incorrect test responses; codes applications according to results. Enters applications or other driver's license or related forms on computer terminal; reviews entry for completeness and accuracy. Operates photographic equipment; prepares photo ID/drivers licenses for receipt of applicant. Balances cash or checks with validation tape totals to assure that all fees are accurately accounted for; prepares deposit records or other routine financial documents necessary to process collected fees; may prepare reports on applications processed. Performs cashiering functions for driver's license fees. In a limited-service facility, reviews, fee checks and checks for necessary attachments the majority of types of motor vehicle registration or title forms; accepts cash or checks for fees and prepares for final processing; issues temporary registration permits. In a full-service motor vehicle facility, reviews, fee checks and checks for necessary attachments, various types of motor vehicle registration or title forms including leased vehicles and dealer and remitter work. Performs other duties as required or assigned.

KNOWLEDGE, SKILLS AND ABILITIES
- Working knowledge of business English, spelling and commercial arithmetic.
- Working knowledge of office methods, practices and procedures.
- Elementary knowledge of basic bookkeeping procedures and techniques.
- Elementary knowledge of the Vehicle Code as it applies to office tasks pertaining to obtaining or retaining a valid driver's license and the processing of various motor vehicle forms.
- Ability to maintain records of some complexity.
- Ability to deal tactfully with the general public and to maintain ,satisfactory
- Working relationships with other employees.
- Ability to communicate both orally and in writing.
- Ability to operate in an independent manner within defined procedures.

SCOPE OF THE EXAMINATION
The written test will cover knowledge, skills, and/or abilities in such areas as:
1. Public and work relations;
2. Telephone etiquette;
3. Records and reports;
4. Vocabulary and spelling;
5. Name and number checking;
6. Filing; and
7. Arithmetic.

HOW TO TAKE A TEST

I. YOU MUST PASS AN EXAMINATION

A. *WHAT EVERY CANDIDATE SHOULD KNOW*

Examination applicants often ask us for help in preparing for the written test. What can I study in advance? What kinds of questions will be asked? How will the test be given? How will the papers be graded?

As an applicant for a civil service examination, you may be wondering about some of these things. Our purpose here is to suggest effective methods of advance study and to describe civil service examinations.

Your chances for success on this examination can be increased if you know how to prepare. Those "pre-examination jitters" can be reduced if you know what to expect. You can even experience an adventure in good citizenship if you know why civil service exams are given.

B. *WHY ARE CIVIL SERVICE EXAMINATIONS GIVEN?*

Civil service examinations are important to you in two ways. As a citizen, you want public jobs filled by employees who know how to do their work. As a job seeker, you want a fair chance to compete for that job on an equal footing with other candidates. The best-known means of accomplishing this two-fold goal is the competitive examination.

Exams are widely publicized throughout the nation. They may be administered for jobs in federal, state, city, municipal, town or village governments or agencies.

Any citizen may apply, with some limitations, such as the age or residence of applicants. Your experience and education may be reviewed to see whether you meet the requirements for the particular examination. When these requirements exist, they are reasonable and applied consistently to all applicants. Thus, a competitive examination may cause you some uneasiness now, but it is your privilege and safeguard.

C. *HOW ARE CIVIL SERVICE EXAMS DEVELOPED?*

Examinations are carefully written by trained technicians who are specialists in the field known as "psychological measurement," in consultation with recognized authorities in the field of work that the test will cover. These experts recommend the subject matter areas or skills to be tested; only those knowledges or skills important to your success on the job are included. The most reliable books and source materials available are used as references. Together, the experts and technicians judge the difficulty level of the questions.

Test technicians know how to phrase questions so that the problem is clearly stated. Their ethics do not permit "trick" or "catch" questions. Questions may have been tried out on sample groups, or subjected to statistical analysis, to determine their usefulness.

Written tests are often used in combination with performance tests, ratings of training and experience, and oral interviews. All of these measures combine to form the best-known means of finding the right person for the right job.

II. HOW TO PASS THE WRITTEN TEST

A. NATURE OF THE EXAMINATION

To prepare intelligently for civil service examinations, you should know how they differ from school examinations you have taken. In school you were assigned certain definite pages to read or subjects to cover. The examination questions were quite detailed and usually emphasized memory. Civil service exams, on the other hand, try to discover your present ability to perform the duties of a position, plus your potentiality to learn these duties. In other words, a civil service exam attempts to predict how successful you will be. Questions cover such a broad area that they cannot be as minute and detailed as school exam questions.

In the public service similar kinds of work, or positions, are grouped together in one "class." This process is known as *position-classification*. All the positions in a class are paid according to the salary range for that class. One class title covers all of these positions, and they are all tested by the same examination.

B. FOUR BASIC STEPS

1) Study the announcement

How, then, can you know what subjects to study? Our best answer is: "Learn as much as possible about the class of positions for which you've applied." The exam will test the knowledge, skills and abilities needed to do the work.

Your most valuable source of information about the position you want is the official exam announcement. This announcement lists the training and experience qualifications. Check these standards and apply only if you come reasonably close to meeting them.

The brief description of the position in the examination announcement offers some clues to the subjects which will be tested. Think about the job itself. Review the duties in your mind. Can you perform them, or are there some in which you are rusty? Fill in the blank spots in your preparation.

Many jurisdictions preview the written test in the exam announcement by including a section called "Knowledge and Abilities Required," "Scope of the Examination," or some similar heading. Here you will find out specifically what fields will be tested.

2) Review your own background

Once you learn in general what the position is all about, and what you need to know to do the work, ask yourself which subjects you already know fairly well and which need improvement. You may wonder whether to concentrate on improving your strong areas or on building some background in your fields of weakness. When the announcement has specified "some knowledge" or "considerable knowledge," or has used adjectives like "beginning principles of..." or "advanced ... methods," you can get a clue as to the number and difficulty of questions to be asked in any given field. More questions, and hence broader coverage, would be included for those subjects which are more important in the work. Now weigh your strengths and weaknesses against the job requirements and prepare accordingly.

3) Determine the level of the position

Another way to tell how intensively you should prepare is to understand the level of the job for which you are applying. Is it the entering level? In other words, is this the position in which beginners in a field of work are hired? Or is it an intermediate or advanced level? Sometimes this is indicated by such words as "Junior" or "Senior" in the class title. Other jurisdictions use Roman numerals to designate the level – Clerk I, Clerk II, for example. The word "Supervisor" sometimes appears in the title. If the level is not indicated by the title, check the description of duties. Will you be working under very close supervision, or will you have responsibility for independent decisions in this work?

4) Choose appropriate study materials

Now that you know the subjects to be examined and the relative amount of each subject to be covered, you can choose suitable study materials. For beginning level jobs, or even advanced ones, if you have a pronounced weakness in some aspect of your training, read a modern, standard textbook in that field. Be sure it is up to date and has general coverage. Such books are normally available at your library, and the librarian will be glad to help you locate one. For entry-level positions, questions of appropriate difficulty are chosen – neither highly advanced questions, nor those too simple. Such questions require careful thought but not advanced training.

If the position for which you are applying is technical or advanced, you will read more advanced, specialized material. If you are already familiar with the basic principles of your field, elementary textbooks would waste your time. Concentrate on advanced textbooks and technical periodicals. Think through the concepts and review difficult problems in your field.

These are all general sources. You can get more ideas on your own initiative, following these leads. For example, training manuals and publications of the government agency which employs workers in your field can be useful, particularly for technical and professional positions. A letter or visit to the government department involved may result in more specific study suggestions, and certainly will provide you with a more definite idea of the exact nature of the position you are seeking.

III. KINDS OF TESTS

Tests are used for purposes other than measuring knowledge and ability to perform specified duties. For some positions, it is equally important to test ability to make adjustments to new situations or to profit from training. In others, basic mental abilities not dependent on information are essential. Questions which test these things may not appear as pertinent to the duties of the position as those which test for knowledge and information. Yet they are often highly important parts of a fair examination. For very general questions, it is almost impossible to help you direct your study efforts. What we can do is to point out some of the more common of these general abilities needed in public service positions and describe some typical questions.

1) General information

Broad, general information has been found useful for predicting job success in some kinds of work. This is tested in a variety of ways, from vocabulary lists to questions about current events. Basic background in some field of work, such as sociology or economics, may be sampled in a group of questions. Often these are principles which have become familiar to most persons through exposure rather than through formal training. It is difficult to advise you how to study for these questions; being alert to the world around you is our best suggestion.

2) Verbal ability

An example of an ability needed in many positions is verbal or language ability. Verbal ability is, in brief, the ability to use and understand words. Vocabulary and grammar tests are typical measures of this ability. Reading comprehension or paragraph interpretation questions are common in many kinds of civil service tests. You are given a paragraph of written material and asked to find its central meaning.

3) **Numerical ability**

Number skills can be tested by the familiar arithmetic problem, by checking paired lists of numbers to see which are alike and which are different, or by interpreting charts and graphs. In the latter test, a graph may be printed in the test booklet which you are asked to use as the basis for answering questions.

4) **Observation**

A popular test for law-enforcement positions is the observation test. A picture is shown to you for several minutes, then taken away. Questions about the picture test your ability to observe both details and larger elements.

5) **Following directions**

In many positions in the public service, the employee must be able to carry out written instructions dependably and accurately. You may be given a chart with several columns, each column listing a variety of information. The questions require you to carry out directions involving the information given in the chart.

6) **Skills and aptitudes**

Performance tests effectively measure some manual skills and aptitudes. When the skill is one in which you are trained, such as typing or shorthand, you can practice. These tests are often very much like those given in business school or high school courses. For many of the other skills and aptitudes, however, no short-time preparation can be made. Skills and abilities natural to you or that you have developed throughout your lifetime are being tested.

Many of the general questions just described provide all the data needed to answer the questions and ask you to use your reasoning ability to find the answers. Your best preparation for these tests, as well as for tests of facts and ideas, is to be at your physical and mental best. You, no doubt, have your own methods of getting into an exam-taking mood and keeping "in shape." The next section lists some ideas on this subject.

IV. KINDS OF QUESTIONS

Only rarely is the "essay" question, which you answer in narrative form, used in civil service tests. Civil service tests are usually of the short-answer type. Full instructions for answering these questions will be given to you at the examination. But in case this is your first experience with short-answer questions and separate answer sheets, here is what you need to know:

1) Multiple-choice Questions

Most popular of the short-answer questions is the "multiple choice" or "best answer" question. It can be used, for example, to test for factual knowledge, ability to solve problems or judgment in meeting situations found at work.

A multiple-choice question is normally one of three types—
- It can begin with an incomplete statement followed by several possible endings. You are to find the one ending which *best* completes the statement, although some of the others may not be entirely wrong.
- It can also be a complete statement in the form of a question which is answered by choosing one of the statements listed.

- It can be in the form of a problem – again you select the best answer.

Here is an example of a multiple-choice question with a discussion which should give you some clues as to the method for choosing the right answer:

When an employee has a complaint about his assignment, the action which will *best* help him overcome his difficulty is to
   A. discuss his difficulty with his coworkers
   B. take the problem to the head of the organization
   C. take the problem to the person who gave him the assignment
   D. say nothing to anyone about his complaint

In answering this question, you should study each of the choices to find which is best. Consider choice "A" – Certainly an employee may discuss his complaint with fellow employees, but no change or improvement can result, and the complaint remains unresolved. Choice "B" is a poor choice since the head of the organization probably does not know what assignment you have been given, and taking your problem to him is known as "going over the head" of the supervisor. The supervisor, or person who made the assignment, is the person who can clarify it or correct any injustice. Choice "C" is, therefore, correct. To say nothing, as in choice "D," is unwise. Supervisors have and interest in knowing the problems employees are facing, and the employee is seeking a solution to his problem.

2) True/False Questions

The "true/false" or "right/wrong" form of question is sometimes used. Here a complete statement is given. Your job is to decide whether the statement is right or wrong.

SAMPLE: A roaming cell-phone call to a nearby city costs less than a non-roaming call to a distant city.

This statement is wrong, or false, since roaming calls are more expensive.

This is not a complete list of all possible question forms, although most of the others are variations of these common types. You will always get complete directions for answering questions. Be sure you understand *how* to mark your answers – ask questions until you do.

V. RECORDING YOUR ANSWERS

Computer terminals are used more and more today for many different kinds of exams.
For an examination with very few applicants, you may be told to record your answers in the test booklet itself. Separate answer sheets are much more common. If this separate answer sheet is to be scored by machine – and this is often the case – it is highly important that you mark your answers correctly in order to get credit.

An electronic scoring machine is often used in civil service offices because of the speed with which papers can be scored. Machine-scored answer sheets must be marked with a pencil, which will be given to you. This pencil has a high graphite content which responds to the electronic scoring machine. As a matter of fact, stray dots may register as answers, so do not let your pencil rest on the answer sheet while you are pondering the correct answer. Also, if your pencil lead breaks or is otherwise defective, ask for another.

Since the answer sheet will be dropped in a slot in the scoring machine, be careful not to bend the corners or get the paper crumpled.

The answer sheet normally has five vertical columns of numbers, with 30 numbers to a column. These numbers correspond to the question numbers in your test booklet. After each number, going across the page are four or five pairs of dotted lines. These short dotted lines have small letters or numbers above them. The first two pairs may also have a "T" or "F" above the letters. This indicates that the first two pairs only are to be used if the questions are of the true-false type. If the questions are multiple choice, disregard the "T" and "F" and pay attention only to the small letters or numbers.

Answer your questions in the manner of the sample that follows:

32. The largest city in the United States is
    A. Washington, D.C.
    B. New York City
    C. Chicago
    D. Detroit
    E. San Francisco

1) Choose the answer you think is best. (New York City is the largest, so "B" is correct.)
2) Find the row of dotted lines numbered the same as the question you are answering. (Find row number 32)
3) Find the pair of dotted lines corresponding to the answer. (Find the pair of lines under the mark "B.")
4) Make a solid black mark between the dotted lines.

VI. BEFORE THE TEST

Common sense will help you find procedures to follow to get ready for an examination. Too many of us, however, overlook these sensible measures. Indeed, nervousness and fatigue have been found to be the most serious reasons why applicants fail to do their best on civil service tests. Here is a list of reminders:

- Begin your preparation early – Don't wait until the last minute to go scurrying around for books and materials or to find out what the position is all about.
- Prepare continuously – An hour a night for a week is better than an all-night cram session. This has been definitely established. What is more, a night a week for a month will return better dividends than crowding your study into a shorter period of time.
- Locate the place of the exam – You have been sent a notice telling you when and where to report for the examination. If the location is in a different town or otherwise unfamiliar to you, it would be well to inquire the best route and learn something about the building.
- Relax the night before the test – Allow your mind to rest. Do not study at all that night. Plan some mild recreation or diversion; then go to bed early and get a good night's sleep.
- Get up early enough to make a leisurely trip to the place for the test – This way unforeseen events, traffic snarls, unfamiliar buildings, etc. will not upset you.
- Dress comfortably – A written test is not a fashion show. You will be known by number and not by name, so wear something comfortable.

- Leave excess paraphernalia at home – Shopping bags and odd bundles will get in your way. You need bring only the items mentioned in the official notice you received; usually everything you need is provided. Do not bring reference books to the exam. They will only confuse those last minutes and be taken away from you when in the test room.
- Arrive somewhat ahead of time – If because of transportation schedules you must get there very early, bring a newspaper or magazine to take your mind off yourself while waiting.
- Locate the examination room – When you have found the proper room, you will be directed to the seat or part of the room where you will sit. Sometimes you are given a sheet of instructions to read while you are waiting. Do not fill out any forms until you are told to do so; just read them and be prepared.
- Relax and prepare to listen to the instructions
- If you have any physical problem that may keep you from doing your best, be sure to tell the test administrator. If you are sick or in poor health, you really cannot do your best on the exam. You can come back and take the test some other time.

VII. AT THE TEST

The day of the test is here and you have the test booklet in your hand. The temptation to get going is very strong. Caution! There is more to success than knowing the right answers. You must know how to identify your papers and understand variations in the type of short-answer question used in this particular examination. Follow these suggestions for maximum results from your efforts:

1) Cooperate with the monitor

The test administrator has a duty to create a situation in which you can be as much at ease as possible. He will give instructions, tell you when to begin, check to see that you are marking your answer sheet correctly, and so on. He is not there to guard you, although he will see that your competitors do not take unfair advantage. He wants to help you do your best.

2) Listen to all instructions

Don't jump the gun! Wait until you understand all directions. In most civil service tests you get more time than you need to answer the questions. So don't be in a hurry. Read each word of instructions until you clearly understand the meaning. Study the examples, listen to all announcements and follow directions. Ask questions if you do not understand what to do.

3) Identify your papers

Civil service exams are usually identified by number only. You will be assigned a number; you must not put your name on your test papers. Be sure to copy your number correctly. Since more than one exam may be given, copy your exact examination title.

4) Plan your time

Unless you are told that a test is a "speed" or "rate of work" test, speed itself is usually not important. Time enough to answer all the questions will be provided, but this does not mean that you have all day. An overall time limit has been set. Divide the total time (in minutes) by the number of questions to determine the approximate time you have for each question.

5) Do not linger over difficult questions

If you come across a difficult question, mark it with a paper clip (useful to have along) and come back to it when you have been through the booklet. One caution if you do this – be sure to skip a number on your answer sheet as well. Check often to be sure that you have not lost your place and that you are marking in the row numbered the same as the question you are answering.

6) Read the questions

Be sure you know what the question asks! Many capable people are unsuccessful because they failed to *read* the questions correctly.

7) Answer all questions

Unless you have been instructed that a penalty will be deducted for incorrect answers, it is better to guess than to omit a question.

8) Speed tests

It is often better NOT to guess on speed tests. It has been found that on timed tests people are tempted to spend the last few seconds before time is called in marking answers at random – without even reading them – in the hope of picking up a few extra points. To discourage this practice, the instructions may warn you that your score will be "corrected" for guessing. That is, a penalty will be applied. The incorrect answers will be deducted from the correct ones, or some other penalty formula will be used.

9) Review your answers

If you finish before time is called, go back to the questions you guessed or omitted to give them further thought. Review other answers if you have time.

10) Return your test materials

If you are ready to leave before others have finished or time is called, take ALL your materials to the monitor and leave quietly. Never take any test material with you. The monitor can discover whose papers are not complete, and taking a test booklet may be grounds for disqualification.

VIII. EXAMINATION TECHNIQUES

1) Read the general instructions carefully. These are usually printed on the first page of the exam booklet. As a rule, these instructions refer to the timing of the examination; the fact that you should not start work until the signal and must stop work at a signal, etc. If there are any *special* instructions, such as a choice of questions to be answered, make sure that you note this instruction carefully.

2) When you are ready to start work on the examination, that is as soon as the signal has been given, read the instructions to each question booklet, underline any key words or phrases, such as *least, best, outline, describe* and the like. In this way you will tend to answer as requested rather than discover on reviewing your paper that you *listed without describing*, that you selected the *worst* choice rather than the *best* choice, etc.

3) If the examination is of the objective or multiple-choice type – that is, each question will also give a series of possible answers: A, B, C or D, and you are called upon to select the best answer and write the letter next to that answer on your answer paper – it is advisable to start answering each question in turn. There may be anywhere from 50 to 100 such questions in the three or four hours allotted and you can see how much time would be taken if you read through all the questions before beginning to answer any. Furthermore, if you come across a question or group of questions which you know would be difficult to answer, it would undoubtedly affect your handling of all the other questions.

4) If the examination is of the essay type and contains but a few questions, it is a moot point as to whether you should read all the questions before starting to answer any one. Of course, if you are given a choice – say five out of seven and the like – then it is essential to read all the questions so you can eliminate the two that are most difficult. If, however, you are asked to answer all the questions, there may be danger in trying to answer the easiest one first because you may find that you will spend too much time on it. The best technique is to answer the first question, then proceed to the second, etc.

5) Time your answers. Before the exam begins, write down the time it started, then add the time allowed for the examination and write down the time it must be completed, then divide the time available somewhat as follows:
    - If 3-1/2 hours are allowed, that would be 210 minutes. If you have 80 objective-type questions, that would be an average of 2-1/2 minutes per question. Allow yourself no more than 2 minutes per question, or a total of 160 minutes, which will permit about 50 minutes to review.
    - If for the time allotment of 210 minutes there are 7 essay questions to answer, that would average about 30 minutes a question. Give yourself only 25 minutes per question so that you have about 35 minutes to review.

6) The most important instruction is to *read each question* and make sure you know what is wanted. The second most important instruction is to *time yourself properly* so that you answer every question. The third most important instruction is to *answer every question*. Guess if you have to but include something for each question. Remember that you will receive no credit for a blank and will probably receive some credit if you write something in answer to an essay question. If you guess a letter – say "B" for a multiple-choice question – you may have guessed right. If you leave a blank as an answer to a multiple-choice question, the examiners may respect your feelings but it will not add a point to your score. Some exams may penalize you for wrong answers, so in such cases *only*, you may not want to guess unless you have some basis for your answer.

7) Suggestions
    a. Objective-type questions
        1. Examine the question booklet for proper sequence of pages and questions
        2. Read all instructions carefully
        3. Skip any question which seems too difficult; return to it after all other questions have been answered
        4. Apportion your time properly; do not spend too much time on any single question or group of questions

5. Note and underline key words – *all, most, fewest, least, best, worst, same, opposite,* etc.
6. Pay particular attention to negatives
7. Note unusual option, e.g., unduly long, short, complex, different or similar in content to the body of the question
8. Observe the use of "hedging" words – *probably, may, most likely,* etc.
9. Make sure that your answer is put next to the same number as the question
10. Do not second-guess unless you have good reason to believe the second answer is definitely more correct
11. Cross out original answer if you decide another answer is more accurate; do not erase until you are ready to hand your paper in
12. Answer all questions; guess unless instructed otherwise
13. Leave time for review

  b. Essay questions
   1. Read each question carefully
   2. Determine exactly what is wanted. Underline key words or phrases.
   3. Decide on outline or paragraph answer
   4. Include many different points and elements unless asked to develop any one or two points or elements
   5. Show impartiality by giving pros and cons unless directed to select one side only
   6. Make and write down any assumptions you find necessary to answer the questions
   7. Watch your English, grammar, punctuation and choice of words
   8. Time your answers; don't crowd material

8) Answering the essay question

Most essay questions can be answered by framing the specific response around several key words or ideas. Here are a few such key words or ideas:

M's: manpower, materials, methods, money, management
P's: purpose, program, policy, plan, procedure, practice, problems, pitfalls, personnel, public relations

  a. Six basic steps in handling problems:
   1. Preliminary plan and background development
   2. Collect information, data and facts
   3. Analyze and interpret information, data and facts
   4. Analyze and develop solutions as well as make recommendations
   5. Prepare report and sell recommendations
   6. Install recommendations and follow up effectiveness

  b. Pitfalls to avoid
   1. *Taking things for granted* – A statement of the situation does not necessarily imply that each of the elements is necessarily true; for example, a complaint may be invalid and biased so that all that can be taken for granted is that a complaint has been registered

2. *Considering only one side of a situation* – Wherever possible, indicate several alternatives and then point out the reasons you selected the best one
3. *Failing to indicate follow up* – Whenever your answer indicates action on your part, make certain that you will take proper follow-up action to see how successful your recommendations, procedures or actions turn out to be
4. *Taking too long in answering any single question* – Remember to time your answers properly

IX. AFTER THE TEST

Scoring procedures differ in detail among civil service jurisdictions although the general principles are the same. Whether the papers are hand-scored or graded by machine we have described, they are nearly always graded by number. That is, the person who marks the paper knows only the number – never the name – of the applicant. Not until all the papers have been graded will they be matched with names. If other tests, such as training and experience or oral interview ratings have been given, scores will be combined. Different parts of the examination usually have different weights. For example, the written test might count 60 percent of the final grade, and a rating of training and experience 40 percent. In many jurisdictions, veterans will have a certain number of points added to their grades.

After the final grade has been determined, the names are placed in grade order and an eligible list is established. There are various methods for resolving ties between those who get the same final grade – probably the most common is to place first the name of the person whose application was received first. Job offers are made from the eligible list in the order the names appear on it. You will be notified of your grade and your rank as soon as all these computations have been made. This will be done as rapidly as possible.

People who are found to meet the requirements in the announcement are called "eligibles." Their names are put on a list of eligible candidates. An eligible's chances of getting a job depend on how high he stands on this list and how fast agencies are filling jobs from the list.

When a job is to be filled from a list of eligibles, the agency asks for the names of people on the list of eligibles for that job. When the civil service commission receives this request, it sends to the agency the names of the three people highest on this list. Or, if the job to be filled has specialized requirements, the office sends the agency the names of the top three persons who meet these requirements from the general list.

The appointing officer makes a choice from among the three people whose names were sent to him. If the selected person accepts the appointment, the names of the others are put back on the list to be considered for future openings.

That is the rule in hiring from all kinds of eligible lists, whether they are for typist, carpenter, chemist, or something else. For every vacancy, the appointing officer has his choice of any one of the top three eligibles on the list. This explains why the person whose name is on top of the list sometimes does not get an appointment when some of the persons lower on the list do. If the appointing officer chooses the second or third eligible, the No. 1 eligible does not get a job at once, but stays on the list until he is appointed or the list is terminated.

X. HOW TO PASS THE INTERVIEW TEST

The examination for which you applied requires an oral interview test. You have already taken the written test and you are now being called for the interview test – the final part of the formal examination.

You may think that it is not possible to prepare for an interview test and that there are no procedures to follow during an interview. Our purpose is to point out some things you can do in advance that will help you and some good rules to follow and pitfalls to avoid while you are being interviewed.

What is an interview supposed to test?

The written examination is designed to test the technical knowledge and competence of the candidate; the oral is designed to evaluate intangible qualities, not readily measured otherwise, and to establish a list showing the relative fitness of each candidate – as measured against his competitors – for the position sought. Scoring is not on the basis of "right" and "wrong," but on a sliding scale of values ranging from "not passable" to "outstanding." As a matter of fact, it is possible to achieve a relatively low score without a single "incorrect" answer because of evident weakness in the qualities being measured.

Occasionally, an examination may consist entirely of an oral test – either an individual or a group oral. In such cases, information is sought concerning the technical knowledges and abilities of the candidate, since there has been no written examination for this purpose. More commonly, however, an oral test is used to supplement a written examination.

Who conducts interviews?

The composition of oral boards varies among different jurisdictions. In nearly all, a representative of the personnel department serves as chairman. One of the members of the board may be a representative of the department in which the candidate would work. In some cases, "outside experts" are used, and, frequently, a businessman or some other representative of the general public is asked to serve. Labor and management or other special groups may be represented. The aim is to secure the services of experts in the appropriate field.

However the board is composed, it is a good idea (and not at all improper or unethical) to ascertain in advance of the interview who the members are and what groups they represent. When you are introduced to them, you will have some idea of their backgrounds and interests, and at least you will not stutter and stammer over their names.

What should be done before the interview?

While knowledge about the board members is useful and takes some of the surprise element out of the interview, there is other preparation which is more substantive. It *is* possible to prepare for an oral interview – in several ways:

1) Keep a copy of your application and review it carefully before the interview

This may be the only document before the oral board, and the starting point of the interview. Know what education and experience you have listed there, and the sequence and dates of all of it. Sometimes the board will ask you to review the highlights of your experience for them; you should not have to hem and haw doing it.

2) Study the class specification and the examination announcement

Usually, the oral board has one or both of these to guide them. The qualities, characteristics or knowledges required by the position sought are stated in these documents. They offer valuable clues as to the nature of the oral interview. For example, if the job involves supervisory responsibilities, the announcement will usually indicate that knowledge of modern supervisory methods and the qualifications of the candidate as a supervisor will be tested. If so, you can expect such questions, frequently in the form of a hypothetical situation which you are expected to solve. NEVER go into an oral without knowledge of the duties and responsibilities of the job you seek.

3) Think through each qualification required

Try to visualize the kind of questions you would ask if you were a board member. How well could you answer them? Try especially to appraise your own knowledge and background in each area, *measured against the job sought*, and identify any areas in which you are weak. Be critical and realistic – do not flatter yourself.

4) Do some general reading in areas in which you feel you may be weak

For example, if the job involves supervision and your past experience has NOT, some general reading in supervisory methods and practices, particularly in the field of human relations, might be useful. Do NOT study agency procedures or detailed manuals. The oral board will be testing your understanding and capacity, not your memory.

5) Get a good night's sleep and watch your general health and mental attitude

You will want a clear head at the interview. Take care of a cold or any other minor ailment, and of course, no hangovers.

What should be done on the day of the interview?

Now comes the day of the interview itself. Give yourself plenty of time to get there. Plan to arrive somewhat ahead of the scheduled time, particularly if your appointment is in the fore part of the day. If a previous candidate fails to appear, the board might be ready for you a bit early. By early afternoon an oral board is almost invariably behind schedule if there are many candidates, and you may have to wait. Take along a book or magazine to read, or your application to review, but leave any extraneous material in the waiting room when you go in for your interview. In any event, relax and compose yourself.

The matter of dress is important. The board is forming impressions about you – from your experience, your manners, your attitude, and your appearance. Give your personal appearance careful attention. Dress your best, but not your flashiest. Choose conservative, appropriate clothing, and be sure it is immaculate. This is a business interview, and your appearance should indicate that you regard it as such. Besides, being well groomed and properly dressed will help boost your confidence.

Sooner or later, someone will call your name and escort you into the interview room. *This is it.* From here on you are on your own. It is too late for any more preparation. But remember, you asked for this opportunity to prove your fitness, and you are here because your request was granted.

What happens when you go in?

The usual sequence of events will be as follows: The clerk (who is often the board stenographer) will introduce you to the chairman of the oral board, who will introduce you to the other members of the board. Acknowledge the introductions before you sit down. Do not be surprised if you find a microphone facing you or a stenotypist sitting by. Oral interviews are usually recorded in the event of an appeal or other review.

Usually the chairman of the board will open the interview by reviewing the highlights of your education and work experience from your application – primarily for the benefit of the other members of the board, as well as to get the material into the record. Do not interrupt or comment unless there is an error or significant misinterpretation; if that is the case, do not hesitate. But do not quibble about insignificant matters. Also, he will usually ask you some question about your education, experience or your present job – partly to get you to start talking and to establish the interviewing "rapport." He may start the actual questioning, or turn it over to one of the other members. Frequently, each member undertakes the questioning on a particular area, one in which he is perhaps most competent, so you can expect each member to participate in the examination. Because time is limited, you may also expect some rather abrupt switches in the direction the questioning takes, so do not be upset by it. Normally, a board member will not pursue a single line of questioning unless he discovers a particular strength or weakness.

After each member has participated, the chairman will usually ask whether any member has any further questions, then will ask you if you have anything you wish to add. Unless you are expecting this question, it may floor you. Worse, it may start you off on an extended, extemporaneous speech. The board is not usually seeking more information. The question is principally to offer you a last opportunity to present further qualifications or to indicate that you have nothing to add. So, if you feel that a significant qualification or characteristic has been overlooked, it is proper to point it out in a sentence or so. Do not compliment the board on the thoroughness of their examination – they have been sketchy, and you know it. If you wish, merely say, "No thank you, I have nothing further to add." This is a point where you can "talk yourself out" of a good impression or fail to present an important bit of information. Remember, *you close the interview yourself*.

The chairman will then say, "That is all, Mr. _____, thank you." Do not be startled; the interview is over, and quicker than you think. Thank him, gather your belongings and take your leave. Save your sigh of relief for the other side of the door.

How to put your best foot forward

Throughout this entire process, you may feel that the board individually and collectively is trying to pierce your defenses, seek out your hidden weaknesses and embarrass and confuse you. Actually, this is not true. They are obliged to make an appraisal of your qualifications for the job you are seeking, and they want to see you in your best light. Remember, they must interview all candidates and a non-cooperative candidate may become a failure in spite of their best efforts to bring out his qualifications. Here are 15 suggestions that will help you:

1) Be natural – Keep your attitude confident, not cocky

If you are not confident that you can do the job, do not expect the board to be. Do not apologize for your weaknesses, try to bring out your strong points. The board is interested in a positive, not negative, presentation. Cockiness will antagonize any board member and make him wonder if you are covering up a weakness by a false show of strength.

2) Get comfortable, but don't lounge or sprawl

Sit erectly but not stiffly. A careless posture may lead the board to conclude that you are careless in other things, or at least that you are not impressed by the importance of the occasion. Either conclusion is natural, even if incorrect. Do not fuss with your clothing, a pencil or an ashtray. Your hands may occasionally be useful to emphasize a point; do not let them become a point of distraction.

3) Do not wisecrack or make small talk

This is a serious situation, and your attitude should show that you consider it as such. Further, the time of the board is limited – they do not want to waste it, and neither should you.

4) Do not exaggerate your experience or abilities

In the first place, from information in the application or other interviews and sources, the board may know more about you than you think. Secondly, you probably will not get away with it. An experienced board is rather adept at spotting such a situation, so do not take the chance.

5) If you know a board member, do not make a point of it, yet do not hide it

Certainly you are not fooling him, and probably not the other members of the board. Do not try to take advantage of your acquaintanceship – it will probably do you little good.

6) Do not dominate the interview

Let the board do that. They will give you the clues – do not assume that you have to do all the talking. Realize that the board has a number of questions to ask you, and do not try to take up all the interview time by showing off your extensive knowledge of the answer to the first one.

7) Be attentive

You only have 20 minutes or so, and you should keep your attention at its sharpest throughout. When a member is addressing a problem or question to you, give him your undivided attention. Address your reply principally to him, but do not exclude the other board members.

8) Do not interrupt

A board member may be stating a problem for you to analyze. He will ask you a question when the time comes. Let him state the problem, and wait for the question.

9) Make sure you understand the question

Do not try to answer until you are sure what the question is. If it is not clear, restate it in your own words or ask the board member to clarify it for you. However, do not haggle about minor elements.

10) Reply promptly but not hastily

A common entry on oral board rating sheets is "candidate responded readily," or "candidate hesitated in replies." Respond as promptly and quickly as you can, but do not jump to a hasty, ill-considered answer.

11) Do not be peremptory in your answers

A brief answer is proper – but do not fire your answer back. That is a losing game from your point of view. The board member can probably ask questions much faster than you can answer them.

12) Do not try to create the answer you think the board member wants

He is interested in what kind of mind you have and how it works – not in playing games. Furthermore, he can usually spot this practice and will actually grade you down on it.

13) Do not switch sides in your reply merely to agree with a board member

Frequently, a member will take a contrary position merely to draw you out and to see if you are willing and able to defend your point of view. Do not start a debate, yet do not surrender a good position. If a position is worth taking, it is worth defending.

14) Do not be afraid to admit an error in judgment if you are shown to be wrong
    The board knows that you are forced to reply without any opportunity for careful consideration. Your answer may be demonstrably wrong. If so, admit it and get on with the interview.

15) Do not dwell at length on your present job
    The opening question may relate to your present assignment. Answer the question but do not go into an extended discussion. You are being examined for a *new* job, not your present one. As a matter of fact, try to phrase ALL your answers in terms of the job for which you are being examined.

Basis of Rating
    Probably you will forget most of these "do's" and "don'ts" when you walk into the oral interview room. Even remembering them all will not ensure you a passing grade. Perhaps you did not have the qualifications in the first place. But remembering them will help you to put your best foot forward, without treading on the toes of the board members.
    Rumor and popular opinion to the contrary notwithstanding, an oral board wants you to make the best appearance possible. They know you are under pressure – but they also want to see how you respond to it as a guide to what your reaction would be under the pressures of the job you seek. They will be influenced by the degree of poise you display, the personal traits you show and the manner in which you respond.

ABOUT THIS BOOK

    This book contains tests divided into Examination Sections. Go through each test, answering every question in the margin. We have also attached a sample answer sheet at the back of the book that can be removed and used. At the end of each test look at the answer key and check your answers. On the ones you got wrong, look at the right answer choice and learn. Do not fill in the answers first. Do not memorize the questions and answers, but understand the answer and principles involved. On your test, the questions will likely be different from the samples. Questions are changed and new ones added. If you understand these past questions you should have success with any changes that arise. Tests may consist of several types of questions. We have additional books on each subject should more study be advisable or necessary for you. Finally, the more you study, the better prepared you will be. This book is intended to be the last thing you study before you walk into the examination room. Prior study of relevant texts is also recommended. NLC publishes some of these in our Fundamental Series. Knowledge and good sense are important factors in passing your exam. Good luck also helps. So now study this Passbook, absorb the material contained within and take that knowledge into the examination. Then do your best to pass that exam.

EXAMINATION SECTION

EXAMINATION SECTION
TEST 1

DIRECTIONS: Each question or incomplete statement is followed by several suggested answers or completions. Select the one that BEST answers the question or completes the statement. *PRINT THE LETTER OF THE CORRECT ANSWER IN THE SPACE AT THE RIGHT.*

1. In public agencies, communications should be based PRIMARILY on a
   A. two-way flow from the top down and from the bottom up, most of which should be given in writing to avoid ambiguity
   B. multi-direction flow among all levels and with outside persons
   C. rapid, internal one-way flow from the top down
   D. two-way flow of information, most of which should be given orally for purposes of clarity

   1.____

2. In some organizations, changes in policy or procedures are often communicated by word of mouth from supervisors to employees with no prior discussion or exchange of viewpoints with employees.
   This procedure often produces employee dissatisfaction CHIEFLY because
   A. information is mostly unusable since a considerable amount of time is required to transmit information
   B. lower-level supervisors tend to be excessively concerned with minor details
   C. management has failed to seek employees' advice before making changes
   D. valuable staff time is lost between decision-making and the implementation of decisions

   2.____

3. For good letter writing, you should try to visualize the person to whom you are writing, especially if you know him.
   Of the following rules, it is LEAST helpful in such visualization to think of
   A. the person's likes and dislikes, his concerns, and his needs
   B. what you would be likely to say if speaking in person
   C. what you would expect to be asked if speaking in person
   D. your official position in order to be certain that your words are proper

   3.____

4. One approach to good informal letter writing is to make letters and conversational.
   All of the following practices will usually help to do this EXCEPT:
   A. If possible, use a style which is similar to the style used when speaking
   B. Substitute phrases for single words (e.g., *at the present time for now*)
   C. Use contractions of words (e.g., *you're* for *you are*)
   D. Use ordinary vocabulary when possible

   4.____

5. All of the following rules will aid in producing clarity in report-writing EXCEPT:
   A. Give specific details or examples, if possible
   B. Keep related words close together in each sentence
   C. Present information in sequential order
   D. Put several thoughts or ideas in each paragraph

6. The one of the following statements about public relations which is MOST accurate is that
   A. in the long run, appearance gains better results than performance
   B. objectivity is decreased if outside public relations consultants are employed
   C. public relations is the responsibility of every employee
   D. public relations should be based on a formal publicity program

7. The form of communication which is usually considered to be MOST personally directed to the intended recipient is the
   A. brochure   B. film   C. letter   D. radio

8. In general, a document that presents an organization's views or opinions on a particular topic is MOST accurately known as a
   A. tear sheet
   B. position paper
   C. flyer
   D. journal

9. Assume that you have been asked to speak before an organization of persons who oppose a newly announced program in which you are involved. You feel tense about talking to this group.
   Which of the following rules generally would be MOST useful in gaining rapport when speaking before the audience?
   A. Impress them with your experience
   B. Stress all areas of disagreement
   C. Talk to the group as to one person
   D. Use formal grammar and language

10. An organization must have an effective public relations program since, at its best, public relations is a bridge to change.
    All of the following statements about communication and human behavior have validity EXCEPT:
    A. People are more likely to talk about controversial matters with like-minded people than with those holding other views
    B. The earlier an experience, the more powerful its effect since it influences how later experiences will be interpreted
    C. In periods of social tension, official sources gain increased believability
    D. Those who are already interested in a topic are the ones who are most open to receive new communications about it

11. An employee should be encouraged to talk easily and frankly when he is dealing with his supervisor.
    In order to encourage such free communication, it would be MOST appropriate for a supervisor to behave in a(n)
    A. sincere manner; assure the employee that you will deal with him honestly and openly
    B. official manner; you are a supervisor and must always act formally with subordinates
    C. investigative manner; you must probe and question to get to a basis of trust
    D. unemotional manner; the employee's emotions and background should play no part in your dealings with him

12. Research findings show that an increase in free communication within an agency GENERALLY results in which one of the following?
    A. Improved morale and productivity
    B. Increased promotional opportunities
    C. An increase in authority
    D. A spirit of honesty

13. Assume that you are a supervisor and your superiors have given you a new-type procedure to be followed.
    Before passing this information on to your subordinates, the one of the following actions that you should take FIRST is to
    A. ask your superiors to send out a memorandum to the entire staff
    B. clarify the procedure in your own mind
    C. set up a training course to provide instruction on the new procedure
    D. write a memorandum to your subordinates

14. Communication is necessary for an organization to be effective.
    The one of the following which is LEAST important for most communication systems is that
    A. messages are sent quickly and directly to the person who needs them to operate
    B. information should be conveyed understandably and accurately
    C. the method used to transmit information should be kept secret so that security can be maintained
    D. senders of messages must know how their messages are received and acted upon

15. Which one of the following is the CHIEF advantage of listening willingly to subordinates and encouraging them to talk freely and honestly?
    It
    A. reveals to supervisors the degree to which ideas that are passed down are accepted by subordinates
    B. reduces the participation of subordinates in the operation of the department
    C. encourages subordinates to try for promotion
    D. enables supervisors to learn more readily what the *grapevine* is saying

16. A supervisor may be informed through either oral or written reports. 16._____
Which one of the following is an ADVANTAGE of using oral reports?
    A. There is no need for a formal record of the report.
    B. An exact duplicate of the report is not easily transmitted to others.
    C. A good oral report requires little time for preparation.
    D. An oral report involves two-way communication between a subordinate and his supervisor.

17. Of the following, the MOST important reason why supervisors should 17._____
communicate effectively with the public is to
    A. improve the public's understanding of information that is important for them to know
    B. establish a friendly relationship
    C. obtain information about the kinds of people who come to the agency
    D. convince the public that services are adequate

18. Supervisors should generally NOT use phrases like *too hard, too easy*, and 18._____
a lot PRINCIPALLY because such phrases
    A. may be offensive to some minority groups
    B. are too informal
    C. mean different things to different people
    D. are difficult to remember

19. The ability to communicate clearly and concisely is an important element in 19._____
effective leadership.
Which of the following statements about oral and written communication is GENERALLY true?
    A. Oral communication is more time-consuming.
    B. Written communication is more likely to be misinterpreted.
    C. Oral communication is useful only in emergencies.
    D. Written communication is useful mainly when giving information to fewer than twenty people.

20. Rumors can often have harmful and disruptive effects on an organization. 20._____
Which one of the following is the BEST way to prevent rumors from becoming a problem?
    A. Refuse to act on rumors, thereby making them less believable.
    B. Increase the amount of information passed along by the *grapevine*.
    C. Distribute as much factual information as possible.
    D. Provide training in report writing.

21. Suppose that a subordinate asks you about a rumor he has heard. The rumor 21._____
deals with a subject which your superiors consider *confidential*.
Which of the following BEST describes how you should answer the subordinate? Tell

A. the subordinate that you don't make the rules and that he should speak to higher ranking officials
B. the subordinate that you will ask your superior for information
C. him only that you cannot comment on the matter
D. him the rumor is not true

22. Supervisors often find it difficult to *get their message across* when instructing newly appointed employees in their various duties.
The MAIN reason for this is generally that the
    A. duties of the employees have increased
    B. supervisor is often so expert in his area that he fails to see it from the learner's point of view
    C. supervisor adapts his instruction to the slowest learner in the group
    D. new employees are younger, less concerned with job security and more interested in fringe benefits

22.____

23. Assume that you are discussing a job problem with an employee under your supervision. During the discussion, you see that the man's eyes are turning away from you and that he is not paying attention.
In order to get the man's attention, you should FIRST
    A. ask him to look you in the eye
    B. talk to him about sports
    C. tell him he is being very rude
    D. change your tone of voice

23.____

24. As a supervisor, you may find it necessary to conduct meetings with your subordinates.
Of the following, which would be MOST helpful in assuring that a meeting accomplishes the purpose for which it was called?
    A. Give notice of the conclusions you would like to reach at the start of the meeting.
    B. Delay the start of the meeting until everyone is present.
    C. Write down points to be discussed in proper sequence.
    D. Make sure everyone is clear on whatever conclusions have been reached and on what must be done after the meeting.

24.____

25. Every supervisor will occasionally be called upon to deliver a reprimand to a subordinate. If done properly, this can greatly help an employee improve his performance.
Which one of the following is NOT a good practice to follow when giving a reprimand?
    A. Maintain your composure and temper
    B. Reprimand a subordinate in the presence of other employees so they can learn the same lesson
    C. Try to understand why the employee was not able to perform satisfactorily
    D. Let your knowledge of the man involved determine the exact nature of the reprimand

25.____

KEY (CORRECT ANSWERS)

1.	C	11.	A
2.	B	12.	A
3.	D	13.	B
4.	B	14.	C
5.	D	15.	A
6.	C	16.	D
7.	C	17.	A
8.	B	18.	C
9.	C	19.	B
10.	C	20.	C

21. B
22. B
23. D
24. D
25. B

TEST 2

DIRECTIONS: Each question or incomplete statement is followed by several suggested answers or completions. Select the one that BEST answers the question or completes the statement. *PRINT THE LETTER OF THE CORRECT ANSWER IN THE SPACE AT THE RIGHT.*

1. Usually one thinks of communication as a single step, essentially that of transmitting an idea.
   Actually, however, this is only part of a total process, the FIRST step of which should be
   A. the prompt dissemination of the idea to those who may be affected by it
   B. motivating those affected to take the required action
   C. clarifying the idea in one's own mind
   D. deciding to whom the idea is to be communicated

2. Research studies on patterns of informal communication have concluded that most individuals in a group tend to be passive recipients of news, while a few make it their business to spread it around in an organization.
   With this conclusion in mind, it would be MOST correct for the supervisor to attempt to identify these few individuals and
   A. give them the complete facts on important matters in advance of others
   B. inform the other subordinates of the identity of these few individuals so that their influence may be minimized
   C. keep them straight on the facts on important matters
   D. warn them to cease passing along any information to others

3. The one of the following which is the PRINCIPAL advantage of making an oral report is that it
   A. affords an immediate opportunity for two-way communication between the subordinate and superior
   B. is an easy method for the superior to use in transmitting information to others of equal rank
   C. saves the time of all concerned
   D. permits more precise pinpointing of praise or blame by means of follow-up questions by the superior

4. An agency may sometimes undertake a public relations program of a defensive nature.
   With reference to the use of defensive public relations, it would be MOST correct to state that it
   A. is bound to be ineffective since defensive statements, even though supported by factual data, can never hope to even partly overcome the effects of prior unfavorable attacks
   B. proves that the agency has failed to establish good relationships with newspapers, radio stations, or other means of publicity

2 (#2)

    C. shows that the upper echelons of the agency have failed to develop sound public relations procedures and techniques
    D. is sometimes required to aid morale by protecting the agency from unjustified criticism and misunderstanding of policies or procedures

5. Of the following factors which contribute to possible undesirable public attitudes towards an agency, the one which is MOST susceptible to being changed by the efforts of the individual employee in an organization is that
    A. enforcement of unpopular regulations as offended many individuals
    B. the organization itself has an unsatisfactory reputation
    C. the public is not interested in agency matters
    D. there are many errors in judgment committed by individual subordinates

6. It is not enough for an agency's services to be of a high quality; attention must also be given to the acceptability of these services to the general public.
This statement is GENERALLY
    A. *false*; a superior quality of service automatically wins public support
    B. *true*; the agency cannot generally progress beyond the understanding and support of the public
    C. *false*; the acceptance by the public of agency services determines their quality
    D. *true*; the agency is generally unable to engage in any effective enforcement activity without public support

7. Sustained agency participation in a program sponsored by a community organization is MOST justified when
    A. the achievement of agency objectives in some area depends partly on the activity of this organization
    B. the community organization is attempting to widen the base of participation in all community affairs
    C. the agency is uncertain as to what the community wants
    D. the agency is uncertain as to what the community wants

8. Of the following, the LEAST likely way in which a records system may serve a supervisor is in
    A. developing a sympathetic and cooperative public attitude toward the agency
    B. improving the quality of supervision by permitting a check on the accomplishment of subordinates
    C. permit a precise prediction of the exact incidences in specific categories for the following year
    D. helping to take the guesswork out of the distribution of the agency

9. Assuming that the *grapevine* in any organization is virtually indestructible, the one of the following which it is MOST important for management to understand is:
    A. What is being spread by means of the *grapevine* and the reason for spreading it
    B. What is being spread by means of the *grapevine* and how it is being spread
    C. Who is involved in spreading the information that is on the *grapevine*
    D. Why those who are involved in spreading the information are doing so

10. When the supervisor writes a report concerning an investigation to which he has been assigned, it should be LEAST intended to provide
    A. a permanent official record of relevant information gathered
    B. a summary of case findings limited to facts which tend to indicate the guilt of a suspect
    C. a statement of the facts on which higher authorities may base a corrective or disciplinary action
    D. other investigators with information so that they may continue with other phases of the investigation

11. In survey work, questionnaires rather than interviews are sometimes used. The one of the following which is a DISADVANTAGE of the questionnaire method as compared with the interview is the
    A. difficulty of accurately interpreting the results
    B. problem of maintaining anonymity of the participant
    C. fact that it is relatively uneconomical
    D. requirement of special training for the distribution of questionnaires

12. in his contacts with the public, an employee should attempt to create a good climate of support for his agency.
    This statement is GENERALLY
    A. *false*; such attempts are clearly beyond the scope of his responsibility
    B. *true*; employees of an agency who come in contact with the public have the opportunity to affect public relations
    C. *false*; such activity should be restricted to supervisors trained in public relations techniques
    D. *true*; the future expansion of the agency depends to a great extent on continued public support of the agency

13. The repeated use by a supervisor of a call for volunteers to get a job done is objectionable MAINLY because it
    A. may create a feeling of animosity between the volunteers and the non-volunteers
    B. may indicate that the supervisor is avoiding responsibility for making assignments which will be most productive
    C. is an indication that the supervisor is not familiar with the individual capabilities of his men
    D. is unfair to men who, for valid reasons, do not, or cannot volunteer

14. Of the following statements concerning subordinates' expressions to a supervisor of their opinions and feelings concerning work situations, the one which is MOST correct is that
    A. by listening and responding to such expressions the supervisor encourages the development of complaints
    B. the lack of such expressions should indicate to the supervisor that there is a high level of job satisfaction
    C. the more the supervisor listens to and responds to such expressions, the more he demonstrates lack of supervisory ability
    D. by listening and responding to such expressions, the supervisor will enable many subordinates to understand and solve their own problems on the job

15. In attempting to motivate employees, rewards are considered preferable to punishment PRIMARILY because
    A. punishment seldom has any effect on human behavior
    B. punishment usually results in decreased production
    C. supervisors find it difficult to punish
    D. rewards are more likely to result in willing cooperation

16. In an attempt to combat the low morale in his organization, a high level supervisor publicized an *open-door policy* to allow employees who wished to do so to come to him with their complaints.
    Which of the following is LEAST likely to account for the fact that no employee came in with a complaint?
    A. Employees are generally reluctant to go over the heads of their immediate supervisor.
    B. The employees did not feel that management would help them.
    C. The low morale was not due to complaints associated with the job.
    D. The employees felt that they had more to lose than to gain.

17. It is MOST desirable to use written instructions rather than oral instructions for a particular job when
    A. a mistake on the job will not be serious
    B. the job can be completed in a short time
    C. there is no need to explain the job minutely
    D. the job involves many details

18. If you receive a telephone call regarding a matter which your office does not handle, you should FIRST
    A. give the caller the telephone number of the proper office so that he can dial again
    B. offer to transfer the caller to the proper office
    C. suggest that the caller re-dial since he probably dialed incorrectly
    D. tell the caller he has reached the wrong office and then hang up

19. When you answer the telephone, the MOST important reason for identifying yourself and your organization is to
    A. give the caller time to collect his or her thoughts
    B. impress the caller with your courtesy
    C. inform the caller that he or she has reached the right number
    D. set a business-like tone at the beginning of the conversation

20. As soon as you pick up the phone, a very angry caller begins immediately to complain about city agencies and *red tape*. He says that he has been shifted to two or three different offices. It turs out that he is seeking information which is not immediately available to you. You believe, you know, however, where it can be found.
    Which of the following actions is the BEST one for you to take?
    A. To eliminate all confusion, suggest that the caller write the agency stating explicitly what he wants.
    B. Apologize by telling the caller how busy city agencies now are, but also tell him directly that you do not have the information he needs.
    C. Ask for the caller's telephone number and assure him you will call back after you have checked further.
    D. Give the caller the name and telephone number of the person who might be able to help, but explain that you are not positive he will get results/

21. Which of the following approaches usually provides the BEST communication in the objectives and values of a new program which is to be introduced?
    A. A general written description of the program by the program manager for review by those who share responsibility
    B. An effective verbal presentation by the program manager to those affected
    C. Development of the plan and operational approach in carrying out the program by the program manager assisted by his key subordinates
    D. Development of the plan by the program manager's supervisor

22. What is the BEST approach for introducing change?
    A
    A. combination of written and also verbal communication to all personnel affected by the change
    B. general bulletin to all personnel
    C. meeting pointing out all the values of the new approach
    D. written directive to key personnel

23. Of the following, committees are BEST used for
    A. advising the head of the organization
    B. improving functional work
    C. making executive decisions
    D. making specific planning decisions

24. An effective discussion leader is one who
    A. announces the problem and his preconceived solution at the start of the discussion
    B. guides and directs the discussion according to pre-arranged outline
    C. interrupts or corrects confused participants to save time
    D. permits anyone to say anything at any time

25. The human relations movement in management theory is basically concerned with
    A. counteracting employee unrest
    B. eliminating the *time and motion* man
    C. interrelationships among individuals in organizations
    D. the psychology of the worker

KEY (CORRECT ANSWERS)

1.	C	11.	A
2.	C	12.	B
3.	A	13.	B
4.	D	14.	D
5.	D	15.	D
6.	B	16.	C
7.	A	17.	D
8.	C	18.	B
9.	A	19.	C
10.	B	20.	C

21. C
22. A
23. A
24. B
25. C

EXAMINATION SECTION
TEST 1

DIRECTIONS: Each question or incomplete statement is followed by several suggested answers or completions. Select the one that BEST answers the question or completes the statement. *PRINT THE LETTER OF THE CORRECT ANSWER IN THE SPACE AT THE RIGHT.*

1. Good procedure in handling complaints from the public may be divided into the following four principal stages:
   I. Investigation of the complaint
   II. Receipt of the complaint
   III. Assignment of responsibility for investigation and correction
   IV. Notification of correction

   The ORDER in which these stages ordinarily come is:
   A. III, II, I, IV   B. II, III, I, IV   C. II, III, IV, I   D. II, IV, III, I

   1.____

2. The department may expect the MOST severe public criticism if
   A. it asks for an increase in its annual budget
   B. it purchases new and costly street cleaning equipment
   C. sanitation officers and men are reclassified to higher salary grades
   D. there is delay in cleaning streets of snow

   2.____

3. The MOST important function of public relations in the department should be to
   A. develop cooperation on the part of the public in keeping streets clean
   B. get stricter penalties enacted for health code violations
   C. recruit candidates for entrance positions who ca be developed into supervisors
   D. train career personnel so that they can advance in the department

   3.____

4. The one of the following which has MOST frequently elicited unfavorable public comment has been
   A. dirty sidewalks or streets   B. dumping on lot
   C. failure to curb dogs   D. overflowing garbage cans

   4.____

5. It has been suggested that, as a public relations measure, sections hold *open house* for the public.
   The MOST effective time for this would be
   A. during the summer when children are not in school and can accompany their parents
   B. during the winter when show is likely to fall and the public can see snow removal preparations
   C. immediately after a heavy snow storm when department snow removal operations are in full progress
   D. when street sanitation is receiving general attention as during *Keep City Clean* week

   5.____

6. When a public agency conducts a public relations program, it is MOST likely to find that each recipient of its message will
   A. disagree with the basic purpose of the message if the officials are not well known to him
   B. accept the message if it is presented by someone perceived as having a definite intention to persuade
   C. ignore the message unless it is presented in a literate and clever manner
   D. give greater attention to certain portions of the message as a result of his individual and cultural differences

7. Following are three statements about public relations and communications:
   I. A person who seeks to influence public opinion can speed up a trend
   II. Mass communications is the exposure of a mass audience to an idea
   III. All media are equally effective in reaching opinion leaders
   Which of the following choices CORRECTLY classifies the above statements into those which are correct and those which are not?
   A. I and II are correct, but III is not.
   B. II and III are correct, but I is not.
   C. I and III are correct, but II is not.
   D. III is correct, but I and II are not.

8. Public relations experts say that MAXIMUM effect for a message results from
   A. concentrating in one medium
   B. ignoring mass media and concentrating on *opinion makers*
   C. presenting only those factors which support a given position
   D. using a combination of two or more of the available media

9. To assure credibility and avoid hostility, the public relations man MUST
   A. make certain his message is truthful, not evasive or exaggerated
   B. make sure his message contains some dire consequence if ignored
   C. repeat the message often enough so that it cannot be ignored
   D. try to reach as many people and groups as possible

10. The public relations man MUST be prepared to assume that members of his audience
    A. may have developed attitudes toward his proposals—favorable, neutral, or unfavorable
    B. will be immediately hostile
    C. will consider his proposals with an open mind
    D. will invariably need an introduction to his subject

11. The one of the following statements that is CORRECT is:
    A. When a stupid question is asked of you by the public, it should be disregarded
    B. If you insist on formality between you and the public, the public will not be able to ask stupid questions that cannot be answered
    C. The public should be treated courteously, regardless of how stupid their questions may be
    D. You should explain to the public how stupid their questions are

12. With regard to public relations, the MOST important item which should be emphasized in an employee training program is that
    A. each inspector is a public relations agent
    B. an inspector should give the public all the information it asks for
    C. it is better to make mistakes and give erroneous information than to tell the public that you do not know the correct answer to their problem
    D. public relations is so specialized a field that only persons specially trained in it should consider it

13. Members of the public frequently ask about departmental procedures.
    Of the following, it is BEST to
    A. advise the public to put the question in writing so that he can get a proper formal reply
    B. refuse to answer because this is a confidential matter
    C. explain the procedure as briefly as possible
    D. attempt to avoid the issue by discussing other matters

14. The effectiveness of a public relations program in a public agency such as the authority is BEST indicated by the
    A. amount of mass media publicity favorable to the policies of the authority
    B. morale of those employees who directly serve the patrons of the authority
    C. public's understanding and support of the authority's program and policies
    D. number of complaint received by the authority from patrons using its facilities

15. In an attempt to improve public opinion about a certain idea, the BEST course of action for an agency to take would be to present the
    A. clearest statements of the idea even though the language is somewhat technical
    B. idea as the result of long-term studies
    C. idea in association with something familiar to most people
    D. idea as the viewpoint of the majority leaders

16. The fundamental factor in any agency's community relations program is
    A. an outline of the objectives
    B. relations with the media
    C. the everyday actions of the employees
    D. a well-planned supervisory program

17. The FUNDAMENTAL factor in the success of a community relations program is
    A. true commitment by the community
    B. true commitment by the administration
    C. a well-planned, systematic approach
    D. the actions of individuals in their contacts with the public

18. The statement below which is LEAST correct is:
    A. Because of selection standards, the supervisor frequently encounters problems resulting from subordinates' inability to express themselves in the language of the profession.
    B. Distortion of the meaning of a communication is usually brought about by a failure to use language that has a precise meaning to others.
    C. The term *filtering* is the distortion or dilution of content of a communication that occurs as information is passed from individual to individual.
    D. The complexity of the *communications net* will directly affect.

19. Consider the following three statements that may or may not be CORRECT:
    I. In order to prevent the stifling of communications flow, supervisors should insist that employees use the formal communications network.
    II. Two-way communications are faster and more accurate than one-way communications.
    III. There is a direct correlation between the effectiveness of communications and the total setting in which they occur.
    The choice below which MOST accurately describes the above statement is:
    A. All three are correct.
    B. All three are incorrect.
    C. More than one statement is correct.
    D. Only one of the statements is correct.

20. The statement below which is MOST inaccurate is:
    A. The supervisor's most important tool in learning whether or not he is communicating well is feedback.
    B. Follow-up is essential if useful feedback is to be obtained.
    C. Subordinates are entitled, as a matter of right, to explanations from management concerning the reasons for orders or directives.
    D. A skilled supervisor is often able to use the grapevine to good advantage.

21. *Since concurrence by those affected is not sought, this kind of communication can be issued with relative ease.*
    The kind of communication being referred to in this quotation is
    A. autocratic   B. democratic   C. directive   D. free-rein

22. The statement below which is LEAST correct is:
    A. Clarity is more important in oral communicating than in written since the readers of a written communication can read it over again.
    B. Excessive use of abbreviations in written communications should be avoided.
    C. Short sentences with simple words are preferred over complex sentences and difficult words in a written communication.
    D. The *newspaper* style of writing ordinarily simplifies expression and facilitates understanding.

5 (#1)

23. Which one of the following is the MOST important factor for the department to consider in building a good public image?
    A. A good working relationship with the news media
    B. An efficient community relations program
    C. An efficient system for handling citizen complaints
    D. The proper maintenance of facilities and equipment
    E. The behavior of individuals in their contacts with the public.

23._____

24. It has been said that the ability to communicate clearly and concisely is the MOST important single skill of the supervisor.
    Consider the following statements:
    I. The adage, *Actions speak louder than words*, has NO application in superior/subordinate communications since good communications are accomplished with words.
    II. The environment in which a communication takes place will *rarely* determine its effect.
    III. Words are symbolic representations which must be associated with past experience or else they are meaningless.
    The choice below which MOST accurately describes the above statements is:
    A. I, II, and III are correct.
    B. I and II are correct, but III is not.
    C. I and III are correct, but II is not.
    D. III is correct, but I and II are not.
    E. I, II, and III are incorrect.

24._____

25. According to expert opinion, the effectiveness of an organization is very dependent upon good upward, downward, and lateral communications. Lateral communications are most important to the activity of coordinating the efforts of organizational units. Before real communication can take place at any level, barriers to communication must be recognized, understood, and removed.
    Consider the following three statements:
    I. The *principal* barrier to good communications is a failure to establish empathy between sender and receiver.
    II. The difference in status or rank between the sender and receiver of a communication may be a communications barrier.
    III. Communications are easier if they travel upward from subordinate to superior
    The choice below which MOST accurately describes the above statements is:
    A. I, II and III are incorrect.   B. I and II are incorrect.
    C. I, II, and III are correct.   D. I and II are correct.
    E. I and III are incorrect.

25._____

KEY (CORRECT ANSWERS)

1.	B	11.	C
2.	D	12.	A
3.	A	13.	C
4.	A	14.	C
5.	D	15.	C
6.	D	16.	C
7.	A	17.	D
8.	D	18.	A
9.	A	19.	D
10.	A	20.	C

21. A
22. A
23. E
24. D
25. E

EXAMINATION SECTION
TEST 1

DIRECTIONS: Each question or incomplete statement is followed by several suggested answers or completions. Select the one that BEST answers the question or completes the statement. *PRINT THE LETTER OF THE CORRECT ANSWER IN THE SPACE AT THE RIGHT.*

1. A multi-line telephone with buttons for eight separate lines, plus a *hold* button, is often used when an office requires more than one outside line.
   If you are talking on one line of this type of office phone when another call comes in, what is the procedure to follow if you want to answer the second call but keep the first call on the line?
   Push the
   A. *hold* button at the same time as you push the *pickup* button of the ringing line
   B. *hold* button and then push the *pickup* button of the ringing line
   C. *pickup* button of the ringing line and then push the *hold* button
   D. *pickup* button of the ringing line and push the *hold* button when you return to the original line

   1._____

2. Suppose that you are asked to prepare a petty cash statement for March. The original and one copy are to go to the personnel office. One copy is to go to the fiscal office, and another copy is to go to your supervisor. The last copy is for your files.
   In preparing the statement and the copies, how many sheets of copy paper should you use?
   A. 3   B. 4   C. 5   D. 8

   2._____

3. Which one of the following is the LEAST important advantage of putting the subject of a letter in the heading to the right of the address? It
   A. makes filing of the copy easier
   B. makes more space available in the body of the letter
   C. simplifies distribution of letters
   D. simplifies determination of the subject of the letter

   3._____

4. Of the following, the MOST efficient way to put 100 copies of a one-page letter into 9½" x 4⅛" envelopes for mailing is to fold _____ into an envelope.
   A. each letter and insert it immediately after folding
   B. each letter separately until all 100 are folded; then insert each one
   C. the 100 letters two at a time, then separate them and insert each one
   D. two letters together, slip them apart, and insert each one

   4._____

5. When preparing papers for filing, it is NOT desirable to
   A. smooth papers that are wrinkled
   B. use paper clips to keep related papers together in the files
   C. arrange the papers in the order in which they will be filed
   D. mend torn papers with cellophane tape

6. Of the following, the BEST reason for a clerical unit to have its own duplicating machine is that the unit
   A. uses many forms which it must reproduce internally
   B. must make two copies of each piece of incoming mail for a special file
   C. must make seven copies of each piece of outgoing mail
   D. must type 200 envelopes each month for distribution to the same offices

7. Several offices use the same photocopying machine.
   If each office must pay its share of the cost of running this machine, the BEST way of determining how much of this cost should be charged to each of these offices is to
   A. determine the monthly number of photocopies made by each office
   B. determine the monthly number of originals submitted for photocopying by each office
   C. determine the number of times per day each office uses the photocopying machine
   D. divide the total cost of running the photocopy machine by the total number of offices using the machine

8. Which one of the following would it be BEST to use to indicate that a file folder has been removed from the files for temporary use in another office?
   A(n)
   A. cross-reference card   B. tickler file marker
   C. aperture card   D. out guide

9. Which one of the following is the MOST important objective of filing?
   A. Giving a secretary something to do in her spare time
   B. Making it possible to locate information quickly
   C. Providing a place to store unneeded documents
   D. Keeping extra papers from accumulating on workers' desks

10. If a check has been made out for an incorrect amount, the BEST action for the writer of the check to take is to
    A. erase the original amount and enter the correct amount
    B. cross out the original amount with a single line and enter the correct amount above it
    C. black out the original amount so that it cannot be read and enter the correct amount above it
    D. write a new check

11. Which one of the following BEST describes the usual arrangement of a tickler file?   11.____
    A. Alphabetical   B. Chronological
    C. Numerical   D. Geographical

12. Which one of the following is the LEAST desirable filing practice?   12.____
    A. Using staples to keep papers together
    B. Filing all material without regard to date
    C. Keeping a record of all materials removed from the files
    D. Writing filing instructions on each paper prior to filing

13. Assume that one of your duties is to keep records of the office supplies used by your unit for the purpose of ordering new supplies when the old supplies run out.   13.____
    The information that will be of MOST help in letting you know when to reorder supplies is the
    A. quantity issued   B. quantity received
    C. quantity on hand   D. stock number

Questions 14-19.

DIRECTIONS: Questions 14 through 19 consist of sets of names and addresses. In each question, the name and address in Column II should be an exact copy of the name and address in Column I. If there is
a mistake *only* in the name, mark your answer A;
a mistake *only* in the address, mark your answer B;
a mistake in *both* name and address, mark your answer C;
no mistake in either name or address, mark your answer D.

SAMPLE QUESTION

Column I
Michael Filbert
456 Reade Street
New York, N.Y. 10013

Column II
Michael Filbert
645 Reade Street
New York, N.Y. 10013

Since there is a mistake only in the address (the street number should be 456 instead of 645), the answer to the sample question is B.

COLUMN I   COLUMN II

14. Esta Wong   Esta Wang   14.____
    141 West 68 St.   141 West 68 St.
    New York, N.Y. 10023   New York,, N.Y. 10023

15. Dr. Alberto Grosso   Dr. Alberto Grosso   15.____
    3475 12th Avenue   3475 12th Avenue
    Brooklyn, N.Y. 11218   Brooklyn, N.Y. 11218

	Column I	Column II	
16.	Mrs. Ruth Bortlas 482 Theresa Ct. Far Rockaway, N.Y. 11691	Ms. Ruth Bortlas 482 Theresa Ct. Far Rockaway, N.Y. 11169	16.____
17.	Mr. and Mrs. Howard Fox 2301 Sedgwick Avenue Bronx, N.Y. 10468	Mr. and Mrs. Howard Fox 231 Sedgwick Ave. Bronx, N.Y. 10458	17.____
18.	Miss Marjorie Black 223 East 23 Street New York, N.Y. 10010	Miss Margorie Black 223 East 23 Street New York, N.Y. 10010	18.____
19.	Michelle Herman 806 Valley Rd. Old Tappan, N.J. 07675	Michelle Hermann 806 Valley Dr. Old Tappan, N.J. 07675	19.____

Questions 20-25.

DIRECTIONS: Questions 20 through 25 are to be answered SOLELY on the basis of the information in the following passage.

Basic to every office is the need for proper lighting. Inadequate lighting is a familiar cause of fatigue and serves to create a somewhat dismal atmosphere in the office. One requirement of proper lighting is that it be of an appropriate intensity. Intensity is measured in foot-candles. According to the Illuminating Engineering Society of New York, for casual seeing tasks such as in reception rooms, inactive file rooms, and other service areas, it is recommended that the amount of light be 30 foot-candles. For ordinary seeing tasks such as reading and work in active file rooms and in mail rooms, the recommended lighting is 100 foot-candles. For very difficult seeing tasks such as accounting, transcribing, and business machine use, the recommended lighting is 150 foot-candles.

Lighting intensity is only one requirement. Shadows and glare are to be avoided. For example, the larger the proportion of a ceiling filled with lighting units, the more glare-free and comfortable the lighting will be. Natural lighting from windows is not too dependable because on dark wintry days, windows yield little usable light, and on sunny afternoons, the glare from windows may be very distracting. Desks should not face the windows. Finally, the main lighting source ought to be overhead and to the left of the user.

20. According to the above passage, insufficient light in the office may cause 20.____
   A. glare B. shadows C. tiredness D. distraction

21. Based on the above passage, which of the following must be considered when planning lighting arrangements? 21.____
   The
   A. amount of natural light present
   B. amount of work to be done
   C. level of difficulty of work to be done
   D. type of activity to be carried out

5 (#1)

22. It can be inferred from the above passage that a well-coordinated lighting scheme is LIKELY to result in
    A. greater employee productivity
    B. elimination of light reflection
    C. lower lighting cost
    D. more use of natural light

    22.____

23. Of the following, the BEST title for the above passage is
    A. Characteristics of Light
    B. Light Measurement Devices
    C. Factors to Consider When Planning Lighting Systems
    D. Comfort vs. Cost When Devising Lighting Arrangements

    23.____

24. According to the above passage, a foot-candle is a measurement of the
    A. number of bulbs used
    B. strength of the light
    C. contrast between glare and shadow
    D. proportion of the ceiling filled with lighting units

    24.____

25. According to the above passage, the number of foot-candles of light that would be needed to copy figures onto a payroll is _____ foot-candles.
    A. less than 30   B. 30   C. 100   D. 150

    25.____

KEY (CORRECT ANSWERS)

1. B	11. B
2. B	12. B
3. B	13. C
4. A	14. A
5. B	15. D
6. A	16. C
7. A	17. B
8. D	18. A
9. B	19. C
10. D	20. C

21. D
22. A
23. C
24. B
25. D

TEST 2

DIRECTIONS: Each question or incomplete statement is followed by several suggested answers or completions. Select the one that BEST answers the question or completes the statement. *PRINT THE LETTER OF THE CORRECT ANSWER IN THE SPACE AT THE RIGHT.*

1. Assume that a supervisor has three subordinates who perform clerical tasks. One of the employees retires and is replaced by someone who is transferred from another unit in the agency. The transferred employee tells the supervisor that she has worked as a clerical employee for two years and understands clerical operations quite well. The supervisor then assigns the transferred employee to a desk, tells the employee to begin working, and returns to his own desk.
The supervisor's action in this situation is
    A. *proper*; experienced clerical employees do not require training when they are transferred to new assignments
    B. *improper*; before the supervisor returns to his desk, he should tell the other two subordinates to watch the transferred employee perform the work
    C. *proper*; if the transferred employee makes any mistakes, she will bring them to the supervisor's attention
    D. *improper*; the supervisor should find out what clerical tasks the transferred employee has performed and give her instruction in those which are new or different

1.____

2. Assume that you are falling behind in completing your work assignments and you believe that your workload is too heavy.
Of the following, the BEST course of action for you to take FIRST is to
    A. discuss the problem with your supervisor
    B. decide which of your assignments can be postponed
    C. try to get some of your co-workers to help you out
    D. plan to take some of the work home with you in order to catch up

2.____

3. Suppose that one of the clerks under your supervision is filling in monthly personnel forms. She asks you to explain a particular personnel regulation which is related to various items on the forms. You are not thoroughly familiar with the regulation.
Of the following responses you may make, the one which will gain the MOST respect from the clerk and which is generally the MOST advisable is to
    A. tell the clerk to do the best she can and that you will check her work later
    B. inform the clerk that you are not sure of a correct explanation but suggest a procedure for her to follow
    C. give the clerk a suitable interpretation so that she will think you are familiar with all regulations
    D. tell the clerk that you will have to read the regulation more thoroughly before you can give her an explanation

3.____

4. Charging out records until a specified due date, with prompt follow-up if they are not returned, is a
   A. *good* idea; it may prevent the records from being kept needlessly on someone's desk for long periods of time
   B. *good* idea; it will indicate the extent of your authority to other departments
   C. *poor* idea; the person borrowing the material may make an error because of the pressure put upon him to return the records
   D. *poor* idea; other departments will feel that you do not trust them with the records and they will be resentful

Questions 5-9.

DIRECTIONS: Questions 5 through 9 consist of three lines of code letters and numbers. The numbers on each line should correspond with the code letters on the same line in accordance with the table below.

Code Letter	P	L	I	J	B	O	H	U	C	G
Corresponding Letter	0	1	2	3	4	5	6	7	8	9

On some of the lines, an error exists in the coding. Compare the letters and numbers in each question carefully. If you find an error or errors on
  only one of the lines in the question, mark your answer A;
  any two lines in the question, mark your answer B;
  all three lines in the question, mark your answer C;
  none of the lines in the question, mark your answer D.

SAMPLE QUESTION
JHOILCP   3652180
BICLGUP   4286970
UCIBHLJ   5824613

In the above sample, the first line is correct since each code letter listed has the correct corresponding number. On the second line, an error exists because code letter L should have the number 1 instead of the number 6. On the third line, an error exists because the code letter U should have the number 7 instead of the number 5. Since there are errors on two of the three lines, the correct answer is B.

5. BULJCIP   4713920
   HIGPOUL   6290571
   OCUHJJBI 5876342

6. CUBLOIJ   8741023
   LCLGCLB   1818914
   JPUHIOC   3076158

7. OIJGCBPO 52398405
   UHPBLIOP 76041250
   CLUIPGPC 81720908

8. BPCOUOJI   40875732
    UOHCIPLB   75682014
    GLHUUCBJ   92677843

9. HOIOHJLH   65256361
    IOJJHHBP   25536640
    OJHBJOPI   53642502

Questions 10-13.

DIRECTIONS: Questions 10 through 13 are to be answered SOLELY on the basis of the information given in the following passage.

The mental attitude of the employee toward safety is exceedingly important in preventing accidents. All efforts designed to keep safety on the employee's mind and to keep accident prevention a live subject in the office will help substantially in a safety program. Although it may seem strange, it is common for people to be careless. Therefore, safety education is a continuous process.

Safety rules should be explained, and the reasons for their rigid enforcement should be given to employees. Telling employees to be careful or giving similar general safety warnings and slogans is probably of little value. Employees should be informed of basic safety fundamentals. This can be done through staff meetings, informal suggestions to employees, movies, and safety instruction cards. Safety instruction cards provide the employees with specific suggestions about safety and serve as a series of timely reminder helping to keep safety on the minds of employees. Pictures, posters, and cartoon sketches on bulletin boards that are located in areas continually used by employees arouse the employees' interest in safety. It is usually good to supplement this type of safety promotion with intensive individual follow-up.

10. The above passage implies that the LEAST effective of the following safety measures is
    A. rigid enforcement of safety rules
    B. getting employees to think in terms of safety
    C. elimination of unsafe conditions in the office
    D. telling employees to stay alert at all times

11. The reason given by the passage for maintaining ongoing safety education is that
    A. people are often careless
    B. office tasks are often dangerous
    C. the value of safety slogans increases with repetition
    D. safety rules change frequently

12. Which one of the following safety aids is MOST likely to be preferred by the passage? A
    A. cartoon of a man tripping over a carton and yelling, *Keep aisles clear!*
    B. poster with a large number one and a caption saying, *Safety First*

C. photograph of a very neatly arranged office
D. large sign with the word THINK in capital letters

13. Of the following, the BEST title for the above passage is   13._____
    A. Basic Safety Fundamentals
    B. Enforcing Safety Among Careless Employees
    C. Attitudes Toward Safety
    D. Making Employees Aware of Safety

Questions 14-21.

DIRECTIONS: Questions 14 through 21 are to be answered SOLELY on the basis of the information and chart given below.

The following chart shows expenses in five selected categories for a one-year period, expressed as percentages of these same expenses during the previous year. The chart compares two different offices. In Office T (represented by ▓▓▓▓), a cost reduction program has been tested for the past year. The other office, Office Q (represented by ▨▨▨▨), served as a control, in that no special effort was made to reduce costs during the past year.

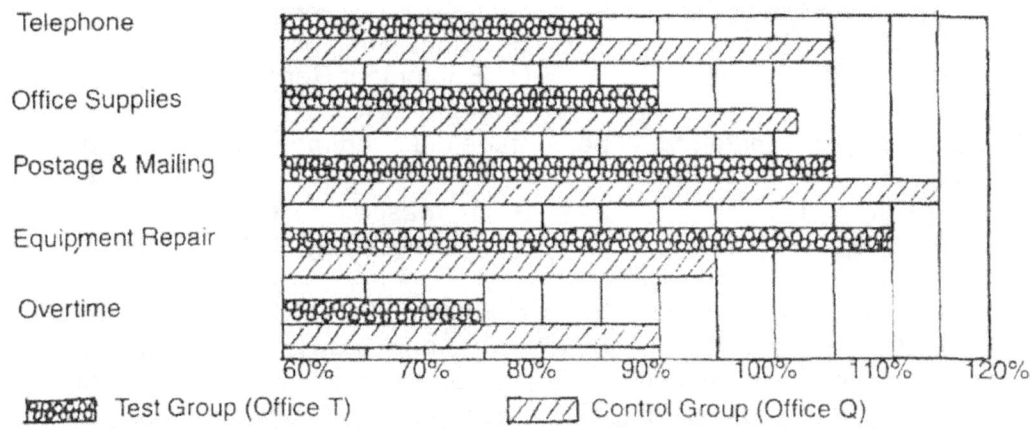

RESULTS OF OFFICE COST REDUCTION PROGRAM
Expenses of Test and Control Groups for 2020
Expressed as Percentages of Same Expenses for 2019

14. In Office T, which category of expense showed the greatest percentage   14._____
    REDUCTION from 2019 to 2020?
    A. Telephone   B. Office Supplies
    C. Postage & Mailing   D. Overtime

15. In which expense category did Office T show the BEST results in percentage   15._____
    terms when compared to Office Q?
    A. Telephone   B. Office Supplies
    C. Postage & Mailing   D. Overtime

16. According to the above chart, the cost reduction program was LEAST effective for the expense category of
    A. Office Supplies
    B. Postage & Mailing
    C. Equipment Repair
    D. Overtime

17. Office T's telephone costs went down during 2020 by approximately how many percentage points?
    A. 15   B. 20   C. 85   D. 104

18. Which of the following changes occurred in expenses for Office Supplies in Office Q in the year 2020 as compared with the year 2019?
    They
    A. increased by more than 100%
    B. remained the same
    C. decreased by a few percentage points
    D. increased by a few percentage points

19. For which of the following expense categories do the results in Office T and the results in Office Q differ MOST NEARLYY by 10 percentage points?
    A. Telephone
    B. Postage & Mailing
    C. Equipment Repair
    D. Overtime

20. In which expense category did Office Q's costs show the GREATEST percentage increase in 2020?
    A. Telephone
    B. Office Supplies
    C. Postage & Mailing
    D. Equipment Repair

21. In Office T, by approximately what percentage did overtime expense change during the past year? It
    A. *increased* by 15%
    B. *increased* by 75%
    C. *decreased* by 10%
    D. *decreased* by 25%

22. In a particular agency, there were 160 accidents in 2017. Of these accidents, 75% were due to unsafe acts and the rest were due to unsafe conditions. In the following year, a special safety program was established. The number of accidents in 2019 due to unsafe acts was reduced to 35% of what it had been in 2017.
    How many accidents due to unsafe acts were there in 2019?
    A. 20   B. 36   C. 42   D. 56

23. At the end of every month, the petty cash fund of Agency A is reimbursed for payments made from the fund during the month. During the month of February, the amounts paid from the fund were entered on receipts as follows: 10 bus fares of $3.50 each and one taxi fare of $35.00. At the end of the month, the money left in the fund was in the following denominations: 15 ten-dollar bills, 10 one-dollar bills, 40 quarters, and 100 dimes.
    If the petty cash fund is reduced by 20% for the following month, how much money will there be available in the petty cash fund for March?
    A. $110.00   B. $200.00   C. $215.00   D. $250.00

24. The one of the following records which it would be MOST advisable to keep in alphabetical order is a
    A. continuous listing of phone messages, including time and caller, for your supervisor
    B. listing of individuals currently employed by your agency in a particular title
    C. record of purchases paid for by the petty cash fund
    D. dated record of employees who have borrowed material from the files in your office

25. Assume that you have been asked to copy by hand a column of numbers with two decimal places from one record to another. Each number consists of three, four, and five digits.
    In order to copy them quickly and accurately, you should copy
    A. each number exactly, making sure that the column of digits farthest to the right is in a straight line and all other columns are lined up
    B. the column of digits farthest to the right and then copy the next column of digits moving from right to left
    C. the column of digits farthest to the left and then copy the next column of digits moving from left to right
    D. the digits to the right of each decimal point and then copy the digits to the left of each decimal point

KEY (CORRECT ANSWERS)

1.	D		11.	A
2.	A		12.	A
3.	D		13.	D
4.	A		14.	D
5.	A		15.	A
6.	C		16.	C
7.	D		17.	A
8.	B		18.	D
9.	C		19.	B
10.	D		20.	C

21. D
22. C
23. B
24. B
25. A

REPORT WRITING
EXAMINATION SECTION
TEST 1

DIRECTIONS: Each question or incomplete statement is followed by several suggested answers or completions. Select the one that BEST answers the question or completes the statement. *PRINT THE LETTER OF THE CORRECT ANSWER IN THE SPACE AT THE RIGHT.*

1. Following are six steps that should be taken in the course of report preparation:
    I. Outlining the material for presentation in the report
    II. Analyzing and interpreting the facts
    III. Analyzing the problem
    IV. Reaching conclusions
    V. Writing, revising, and rewriting the final copy
    VI. Collecting data

    According to the principles of good report writing, the CORRECT order in which these steps should be taken is:
    A. VI, III, II, I, IV, V
    B. III, VI, II, IV, I, V
    C. III, VI, II, I, IV, V
    D. VI, II, III, IV, I, V

    1._____

2. Following are three statements concerning written reports:
    I. Clarity is generally more essential in oral reports than in written reports.
    II. Short sentences composed of simple words are generally preferred to complex sentences and difficult words.
    III. Abbreviations may be used whenever they are customary and will not distract the attention of the reader.

    Which of the following choices correctly classifies the above statements in to those which are valid and those which are not valid?
    A. I and II are valid, but III is not valid
    B. I is valid, but II and III are not valid.
    C. II and III are valid, but I is not valid.
    D. III is valid, but I and II are not valid.

    2._____

3. In order to produce a report written in a style that is both understandable and effective, an investigator should apply the principles of unit, coherence, and emphasis.
    The one of the following which is the BEST example of the principle of coherence is
    A. interlinking sentences so that thoughts flow smoothly
    B. having each sentence express a single idea to facilitate comprehension
    C. arranging important points in prominent positions so they are not overlooked
    D. developing the main idea fully to insure complete consideration

    3._____

31

4. Assume that a supervisor is preparing a report recommending that a standard work procedure be changed.
   Of the following, the MOST important information that he should include in this report is
   A. a complete description of the present procedure
   B. the details and advantages of the recommended procedure
   C. the type and amount of retraining needed
   D. the percentage of men who favor the change

5. When you include in your report on an inspection some information which you have obtained from other individuals, it is MOST important that
   A. this information have no bearing on the work these other people are performing
   B. you do not report as fact the opinions of other individuals
   C. you keep the source of the information confidential
   D. you do not tell the other individuals that their statements will be included in your report

6. Before turning in a report of an investigator of an accident, you discover some additional information you did not know about when you wrote the report. Whether or not you re-write your report to include this additional information should depend MAINLY on the
   A. source of this additional information
   B. established policy covering the subject matter of the report
   C. length of the report and the time it would take you to re-write it
   D. bearing this additional information will have on the conclusions in the report

7. The MOST desirable *first* step in the planning of a written report is to
   A. ascertain what necessary information is readily available in the files
   B. outline the methods you will employ to get the necessary information
   C. determine the objectives and uses of the report
   D. estimate the time and cost required to complete the report

8. In writing a report, the practice of taking up the least important points and the most important points last is a
   A. *good* technique since the final points made in a report will make the greatest impression on the reader
   B. *good* technique since the material is presented in a more logical manner and will lead directly to the conclusions
   C. *poor* technique since the reader's time is wasted by having to review irrelevant information before finishing the report
   D. *poor* technique since it may cause the reader to lose interest in the report and arrive at incorrect conclusions about the report

3 (#1)

9. Which one of the following serves as the BEST guideline for you to follow for effective written reports?
Keep sentences
   A. short and limit sentences to one thought
   B. short and use as many thoughts as possible
   C. long and limit sentences to one thought
   D. long and use as many thoughts as possible

9.____

10. One method by which a supervisor might prepare written reports to management is to begin with the conclusions, results, or summary, and to follow this with the supporting data.
The BEST reason why management may *prefer* this form of report is that
   A. management lacks the specific training to understand the data
   B. the data completely supports the conclusions
   C. time is saved by getting to the conclusions of the report first
   D. the data contains all the information that is required for making the conclusions

10.____

11. When making written reports, it is MOST important that they be
   A. well-worded   B. accurate as to the facts
   C. brief   D. submitted immediately

11.____

12. Of the following, the MOST important reason for a supervisor to prepare good written reports is that
   A. a supervisor is rated on the quality of his reports
   B. decisions are often made on the basis of the reports
   C. such reports take less time for superiors to review
   D. such reports demonstrate efficiency of department operations

12.____

13. Of the following, the BEST test of a good report is whether it
   A. provides the information needed
   B. shows the good sense of the writer
   C. is prepared according to a proper format
   D. is grammatical and neat

13.____

14. When a supervisor writes a report, he can BEST show that he has a understanding of the subject of the report by
   A. including necessary facts and omitting nonessential details
   B. using statistical data
   C. giving his conclusions but not the data on which they are based
   D. using a technical vocabulary

14.____

15. Suppose you and another supervisor on the same level are assigned to work together on a report. You disagree strongly with one of the recommendations the other supervisor wants to include in the report but you cannot change his views.

15.____

33

Of the following, it would be BEST that
- A. you refuse to accept responsibility for the report
- B. you ask that someone else be assigned to this project to replace you
- C. each of you state his own ideas about this recommendation in the report
- D. you give in to the other supervisor's opinion for the sake of harmony

16. Standardized forms are often provided for submitting reports. 16.____
   Of the following, the MOST important advantage of using standardized forms for reports is that
   - A. they take less time to prepare than individually written reports
   - B. the person making the report can omit information he considers unimportant
   - C. the responsibility for preparing these reports can be turned over to subordinates
   - D. necessary information is less likely to be omitted

17. A report which may BEST be classed as a *periodic* report is one which 17.____
   - A. requires the same type of information at regular intervals
   - B. contains detailed information which is to be retained in permanent records
   - C. is prepared whenever a special situation occurs
   - D. lists information in graphic form

18. In the writing of reports or letters, the ideas presented in a paragraph are usually of unequal importance and require varying degrees of emphasis. 18.____
   All of the following are methods of placing extra stress on an idea EXCEPT
   - A. repeating it in a number of forms
   - B. placing it in the middle of the paragraph
   - C. placing it either at the beginning or at the end of a paragraph
   - D. underlining it

Questions 19-25.

DIRECTIONS: Questions 19 through 25 concern the subject of report writing and are based on the information and incidents described in the following paragraph. (In answering these questions, assume that the facts and incidents in the paragraph are true.)

On December 15, at 8 A.M., seven Laborers reported to Foreman Joseph Meehan in the Greenbranch Yard in Queens. Meehan instructed the men to load some 50-pound boxes of books on a truck for delivery to an agency building in Brooklyn. Meehan told the men that, because the boxes were rather heavy, two men should work together, helping each other lift and load each box. Since Michael Harper, one of the Laborers, was without a partner, Meehan helped him with the boxes for a while. When Meehan was called to the telephone in a nearby building, however, Harper decided to lift a box himself. He appeared able to lift the box, but, as he got the box halfway up, he cried out that he had a sharp pain in his back. Another Laborer, Jorge Ortiz, who was passing by, ran over to help Harper put the box down. Harper suddenly dropped the box, which fell on Ortiz' right foot. By this time, Meehan had come out of the building. He immediately helped get the box off Ortiz' foot and had both men lie down. Meehan covered the men with blankets and called an ambulance, which arrived a half hour later. At the hospital, the doctor said that the X-ray results showed that Ortiz' right foot was broken in three places.

19. What would be the BEST term to use in a report describing the injury of Jorge Ortiz? 19.____
    A. Strain   B. Fracture   C. Hernia   D. Hemorrhage

20. Which of the following would be the MOST accurate summary for the Foreman to put in his report of the incident? 20.____
    A. Ortiz attempted to help Harper carry a box which was too heavy for one person, but Harper dropped it before Ortiz got there.
    B. Ortiz tried to help Harper carry a box but Harper got a pain in his back and accidentally dropped the box on Ortiz' foot.
    C. Harper refused to follow Meehan's orders and lifted a box too heavy for him; he deliberately dropped it when Ortiz tried to help him carry it.
    D. Harper lifted a box and felt a pain in his back; Ortiz tried to help Harper put the box down but Harper accidentally dropped it on Ortiz' foot.

21. One of the Laborers at the scene of the accident was asked his version of the incident. 21.____
    Which information obtained from this witness would be LEAST important for including in the accident report?
    A. His opinion as to the cause of the accident
    B. How much of the accident he saw
    C. His personal opinion of the victims
    D. His name and address

22. What should be the MAIN objective of writing a report about the incident described in the above paragraph? To 22.____
    A. describe the important elements in the accident situation
    B. recommend that such Laborers as Ortiz be advised not to interfere in another's work unless given specific instructions
    C. analyze the problems occurring when there are not enough workers to perform a certain task
    D. illustrate the hazards involved in performing routine everyday tasks

23. Which of the following is information *missing* from the above passage but which *should* be included in a report of the incident? The 23.____
    A. name of the Laborer's immediate supervisor
    B. contents of the boxes
    C. time at which the accident occurred
    D. object or action that caused the injury to Ortiz' foot

24. According to the description of the incident, the accident occurred because 24.____
    A. Ortiz attempted to help Harper who resisted his help
    B. Harper failed to follow instructions given him by Meehan
    C. Meehan was not supervising his men as closely as he should have
    D. Harper was not strong enough to carry the box once he lifted it

25. Which of the following is MOST important for a foreman to avoid when writing up an official accident report?   25._____
    A. Using technical language to describe equipment involved in the accident
    B. Putting in details which might later be judged unnecessary
    C. Giving an opinion as to conditions that contributed to the accident
    D. Recommending discipline for employees who, in his opinion, caused the accident

KEY (CORRECT ANSWERS)

1.	B		11.	B
2.	C		12.	B
3.	A		13.	A
4.	B		14.	A
5.	B		15.	C
6.	D		16.	D
7.	C		17.	A
8.	D		18.	B
9.	A		19.	B
10.	C		20.	D

21. C
22. A
23. C
24. B
25. D

TEST 2

DIRECTIONS: Each question or incomplete statement is followed by several suggested answers or completions. Select the one that BEST answers the question or completes the statement. *PRINT THE LETTER OF THE CORRECT ANSWER IN THE SPACE AT THE RIGHT.*

1. Lieutenant X is preparing a report to submit to his commanding officer in order to get approval of a plan of operation he has developed.
   The report starts off with the statement of the problem and continues with the details of the problem. It contains factual information gathered with the help of field and operational personnel. It contains a final conclusion and recommendation for action. The recommendation is supplemented by comments from other precinct staff members on how the recommendations will affect their areas of responsibility. The report also includes directives and general orders ready for the commanding officer's signature. In addition, it has two statements of objections presented by two precinct staff members.
   Which one of the following, if any, is either an item that Lieutenant X should have included in his report and which is not mentioned above, or is an item which Lieutenant X improperly did include in his report?
      A. Considerations of alternative courses of action and their consequences should have been covered in the report.
      B. The additions containing undocumented objections to the recommended course of action should not have been included as part of the report.
      C. A statement on the qualifications of Lieutenant X, which would support his expertness in the field under consideration, should have been included in the report.
      D. The directives and general orders should not have been prepared and included in the report until the commanding officer had approved the recommendations.
      E. None of the above, since Lieutenant X's report was both proper and complete.

1.____

2. During a visit to a section, the district supervisor criticizes the method being used by the assistant foreman to prepare a certain report and orders him to modify the method. This change ordered by the district supervisor is in direct conflict with the specific orders of the foreman.
   In this situation, it would be BEST for the assistant foreman to
      A. change the method and tell the foreman about the change at the first opportunity
      B. change the method and rely on the district supervisor to notify the foreman
      C. report the matter to the foreman and delay the preparation of the report
      D. ask the district supervisor to discuss the matter with the foreman but use the old method for the time being

2.____

3. A department officer should realize that the MOST usual reason for writing a report is to
   A. give orders and follow up their execution
   B. establish a permanent record
   C. raise questions
   D. supply information

4. A very important report which is being prepared by a department officer will soon be due on the desk of the district supervisor. No typing help is available at this time for the officer.
   For the officer to write out this report in longhand in such a situation would be
   A. *bad*; such a report would not make the impression a typed report would
   B. *good*; it is important to get the report in on time
   C. *bad*; the district supervisor should not be required to read longhand reports
   D. *good*; it would call attention to the difficult conditions under which this section must work

5. In a well-written report, the length of each paragraph in the report should be
   A. varied according to the content
   B. not over 300 words
   C. pretty nearly the same
   D. gradually longer as the report is developed and written

6. A clerk in the headquarters office complains to you about the way in which you are filing out a certain report.
   It would be BEST for you to
   A. tell the clerk that you are following official procedures in filling out the report
   B. ask to be referred to the clerk's superior
   C. ask the clerk exactly what is wrong with the way in which you are filling out the report
   D. tell the clerk that you are following the directions of the district supervisor

7. The use of an outline to help in writing a report is
   A. *desirable*, in order to insure good organization and coverage
   B. *necessary*, so it can be used as an introduction to the report itself
   C. *undesirable*, since it acts as a straightjacket and may result in an unbalanced report
   D. *desirable*, if you know your immediate supervisor reads reports with extreme care and attention

8. It is advisable that a department officer do his paper work and report writing as soon as he has completed an inspection MAINLY because
   A. there are usually deadlines to be met
   B. it insures a steady work-flow
   C. he may not have time for this later
   D. the facts are then freshest in his mind

9. Before you turn in a report you have written of an investigation that you have made, you discover some additional information you didn't know about before. Whether or not you re-write the report to include this additional information should depend MAINLY on the
   A. amount of time remaining before the report is due
   B. established policy of the department covering the subject matter of the report
   C. bearing this information will have on the conclusions of the report
   D. number of people who will eventually review the report

10. When a supervisory officer submits a periodic report to the district supervisor, he should realize that the CHIEF importance of such a report is that it
    A. is the principal method of checking on the efficiency of the supervisor and his subordinates
    B. is something to which frequent reference will be made
    C. eliminates the need for any personal follow-up or inspection by higher echelons
    D. permits the district supervisor to exercise his functions of direction, supervision, and control better

11. Conclusions and recommendations are usually placed at the end rather than at the beginning of a report because
    A. the person preparing the report may decide to change some of the conclusions and recommendations before he reaches the end of the report
    B. they are the most important part of the report
    C. they can be judged better by the person to whom the report is sent after he reads the facts and investigators which come earlier in the report
    D. they can be referred to quickly when needed without reading the rest of the report

12. The use of the same method of record-keeping and reporting by all agency sections is
    A. *desirable*, MAINLY because it saves time in section operations
    B. *undesirable*, MAINLY because it kills the initiative of the individual section foreman
    C. *desirable*, MAINLY because it will be easier for the administrator to evaluate and compare section operations
    D. *undesirable*, MAINLY because operations vary from section to section and uniform record-keeping and reporting is not appropriate

13. The GREATEST benefit the section officer will have from keeping complete and accurate records and reports of section operations is that
    A. he will find it easier to run his section efficiently
    B. he will need less equipment
    C. he will need less manpower
    D. the section will run smoothly when he is out

14. You have prepared a report to your superior and are ready to send it forward. 14.____
But on re-reading it, you think some parts are not clearly expressed and your
superior ay have difficulty getting your point.
Of the following, it would be BEST for you to
    A. give the report to one of your men to read, and if he has no trouble
       understanding it send it through
    B. forward the report and call your superior the next day to ask whether it
       was all right
    C. forward the report as is; higher echelons should be able to understand
       any report prepared by a section officer
    D. do the report over, re-writing the sections you are in doubt about

15. The BEST of the following statements concerning reports is that 15.____
    A. a carelessly written report may give the reader an impression of
       inaccuracy
    B. correct grammar and English are unimportant if the main facts are given
    C. every man should be required to submit a daily work report
    D. the longer and more wordy a report is, the better it will read

16. In writing a report, the question of whether or not to include certain material 16.____
could be determined BEST by considering the
    A. amount of space the material will occupy in the report
    B. amount of time to be spent in gathering the material
    C. date of the material
    D. value of the material to the superior who will read the report

17. Suppose you are submitting a fairly long report to your superior. 17.____
The one of the following sections that should come FIRST in this report is a
    A. description of how you gathered material
    B. discussion of possible objections to your recommendations
    C. plan of how your recommendations can be put into practice
    D. statement of the problem dealt with

Questions 18-20.

DIRECTIONS: A foreman is asked to write a report on the incident described in the following
passage. Answer Questions 18 through 20 based on the following information.

On March 10, Henry Moore, a laborer, was in the process of transferring some equipment from the machine shop to the third floor. He was using a dolly to perform this task and, as he was wheeling the material through the machine shop, laborer Bob Greene called to him. As Henry turned to respond to Bob, he jammed the dolly into Larry Mantell's leg, knocking Larry down in the process and causing the heavy drill that Larry was holding to fall on Larry's foot. Larry started rubbing his foot and then, infuriated, jumped up and punched Henry in the jaw. The force of the blow drove Henry's head back against the wall. Henry did not fight back; he appeared to be dazed. An ambulance was called to take Henry to the hospital, and the ambulance attendant told the foreman that it appeared likely that Henry had suffered a concussion. Larry's injuries consisted of some bruises, but he refused medical attention.

18. An adequate report of the above incident should give as minimum information the names of the persons involved, the names of the witnesses, the date and the time that each event took place, and the

    A. names of the ambulance attendants
    B. names of all the employees working in the machine shop
    C. location where the accident occurred
    D. nature of the previous safety training each employee had been given

18._____

19. The only one of the following which is NOT a fact is

    A. Bob called to Henry
    B. Larry suffered a concussion
    C. Larry rubbed his foot
    D. the incident took place in the machine shop

19._____

20. Which of the following would be the MOST accurate summary of the incident for the foreman to put in his report of the accident?

    A. Larry Mantell punched Henry Moore because a drill fell on his foot and he was angry. Then Henry fell and suffered a concussion.
    B. Henry Moore accidentally jammed a dolly into Larry Mantell's foot, knocking Larry down. Larry punched Henry, pushing him into the wall and causing him to bang his head against the wall.
    C. Bob Greene called Henry Moore. A dolly than jammed into Larry Mantell and knocked him down. Larry punched Henry who tripped and suffered some bruises. An ambulance was called.
    D. A drill fell on Larry Mantell's foot. Larry jumped up suddenly and punched Henry Moore and pushed him into the wall. Henry may have suffered a concussion as a result of falling.

20._____

Questions 21-25.

DIRECTIONS: Questions 21 through 25 are to be answered ONLY on the basis of the information provided in the following passage.

A written report is a communication of information from one person to another. It is an account of some matter especially investigated, however routine that matter may be. The ultimate basis of any good written report is facts, which become known through observation and verification. Good written reports may seem to be no more than general ideas and opinions. However, in such cases, the facts leading to these opinions were gathered, verified, and reported earlier, and the opinions are dependent upon these facts. Good style, proper form, and emphasis cannot make a good written report out of unreliable information and bad judgment; but, on the other hand, solid investigation and brilliant thinking are not likely to become very useful until they are effectively communicated to others. If a person's work calls for written reports, then his work is often no better than his written reports.

21. Based on the information in the above passage, it can be concluded that opinions expressed in a report should be
    A. based on facts which are gathered and reported
    B. emphasized repeatedly when they result from a special investigation
    C. kept to a minimum
    D. separated from the body of the report

    21._____

22. In the above passage, the one of the following which is mentioned as a way of establishing facts is
    A. authority
    B. communication
    C. reporting
    D. verification

    22._____

23. According to the above passage, the characteristic shared by ALL written reports is that they are
    A. accounts of routine matters
    B. transmissions of information
    C. reliable and logical
    D. written in proper form

    23._____

24. Which of the following conclusions can logically be drawn from the information given in the above passage?
    A. Brilliant thinking can make up for unreliable information in a report.
    B. One method of judging an individual's work is the quality of the written reports he is required to submit.
    C. Proper form and emphasis can make a good report out of unreliable information.
    D. Good written reports that seem to be no more than general ideas should be rewritten.

    24._____

25. Which of the following suggested titles would be MOST appropriate for this passage?
    A. Gathering and Organizing Facts
    B. Techniques of Observation
    C. Nature and Purpose of Reports
    D. Reports and Opinions: Differences and Similarities

    25._____

KEY (CORRECT ANSWERS)

1.	A		11.	C
2.	A		12.	C
3.	D		13.	A
4.	B		14.	D
5.	A		15.	A
6.	C		16.	D
7.	A		17.	D
8.	D		18.	C
9.	C		19.	B
10.	D		20.	B

21. A
22. D
23. B
24. B
25. C

TEST 3

DIRECTIONS: Each question or incomplete statement is followed by several suggested answers or completions. Select the one that BEST answers the question or completes the statement. *PRINT THE LETTER OF THE CORRECT ANSWER IN THE SPACE AT THE RIGHT.*

Questions 1-5.

DIRECTIONS: The following is an accident report similar to those used in departments for reporting accidents. Questions 1 through 5 are be answered using ONLY the information given in this report.

ACCIDENT REPORT

FROM: John Doe	DATE OF REPORT: June 23	
TITLE: Sanitation Worker		
DATE OF ACCIDENT: June 22 time 3 AM PM	CITY: Metropolitan	
PLACE: 1489 Third Avenue		
VEHICLE NO. 1	VEHICLE NO. 2	
OPERATOR: John Doe, Sanitation Worker Title	OPERATOR: Richard Roe	
VEHICLE CODE NO: 14-238	ADDRESS: 498 High Street	
LICENSE NO.: 0123456	OWNER: Henry Roe ADDRESS: 786 E.83 St.	LIC. NO.: 5N1492
DESCRIPTION OF ACCIDENT: Light green Chevrolet sedan while trying to pass drove in to rear side of sanitation truck which had stopped to collect garbage. No one was injured but there was property damage.		
NATURE OF DAMAGE TO PRIVATE VEHICLE: Right front fender crushed, bumper bent		
DAMAGE TO CITY VEHICLE: Front of left rear fender pushed in. Paint scraped.		
NAME OF WITNESS: Frank Brown	ADDRESS: 48 Kingsway	
SIGNATURE OF PERSON MAKING THIS REPORT *John Doe*	BADGE NO.: 428	

1. Of the following, the one which has been omitted from this accident report is the 1.____
   A. location of the accident
   B. drivers of the vehicles involved
   C. traffic situation at the time of the accident
   D. owners of the vehicles involved

2. The address of the driver of Vehicle No. 1 is not required because he 2.____
   A. is employed by the department   B. is not the owner of the vehicle
   C. reported the accident   D. was injured in the accident

3. The report indicates that the driver of Vehicle No. 2 was PROBABLY 3.____
   A. passing on the wrong side of the truck
   B. not wearing his glasses
   C. not injured in the accident
   D driving while intoxicated

44

4. The number of people *specifically* referred to in this report is
   A. 3   B. 4   C. 5   D. 6

5. The license number of Vehicle No. 1 is
   A. 428   B. 5N1492   C. 14-238   D. 0123456

6. In a report of unlawful entry into department premises, it is LEAST important to include the
   A. estimated value of the property missing
   B. general description of the premises
   C. means used to get into the premises
   D. time and date of entry

7. In a report of an accident, it is LEAST important to include the
   A. name of the insurance company of the person injured in the accident
   B. probable cause of the accident
   C. time and place of the accident
   D. names and addresses of all witnesses of the accident

8. Of the following, the one which is NOT required in the preparation of a weekly functional expense report is the
   A. hourly distribution of the time by proper heading in accordance with the actual work performed
   B. signatures of officers not involved in the preparation of the report
   C. time records of the men who appear on the payroll of the respective locations
   D. time records of men working in other districts assigned to this location

KEY (CORRECT ANSWERS)

1. C   5. D
2. A   6. B
3. C   7. A
4. B   8. B

RECORD KEEPING
EXAMINATION SECTION
TEST 1

DIRECTIONS: Each question or incomplete statement is followed by several suggested answers or completions. Select the one that BEST answers the question or completes the statement. *PRINT THE LETTER OF THE CORRECT ANSWER IN THE SPACE AT THE RIGHT.*

Questions 1-15.

DIRECTIONS: Questions 1 through 15 are to be answered on the basis of the following list of company names below. Arrange a file alphabetically, word-by-word, disregarding punctuation, conjunctions, and apostrophes. Then answer the questions.

    A Bee C Reading Materials
    ABCO Parts
    A Better Course for Test Preparation
    AAA Auto Parts Co.
    A-Z Auto Parts, Inc.
    Aabar Books
    Abbey, Joanne
    Boman-Sylvan Law Firm
    BMW Autowerks
    C Q Service Company
    Chappell-Murray, Inc.
    E&E Life Insurance
    Emcrisco
    Gigi Arts
    Gordon, Jon & Associates
    SOS Plumbing
    Schmidt, J.B. Co.

1. Which of these files should appear FIRST? 1.____
   A. ABCO Parts
   B. A Bee C Reading Materials
   C. A Better Course for Test Preparation
   D. AAA Auto Parts Co.

2. Which of these files should appear SECOND? 2.____
   A. A-Z Auto Parts, Inc.
   B. A Bee C Reading Materials
   C. A Better Course for Test Preparation
   D. AAA Auto Parts Co.

2 (#1)

3. Which of these files should appear THIRD? 3.____
   A. ABCO Parts
   B. A Bee C Reading Materials
   C. Aabar Books
   D. AAA Auto Parts Co.

4. Which of these files should appear FOURTH? 4.____
   A. Aabar Books
   B. ABCO Parts
   C. Abbey, Joanne
   D. AAA Auto Parts Co.

5. Which of these files should appear LAST? 5.____
   A. Gordon, Jon & Associates
   B. Gigi Arts
   C. Schmidt, J.B. Co.
   D. SOS Plumbing

6. Which of these files should appear between A-Z Auto Parts, Inc. and Abbey, Joanne? 6.____
   A. A Bee C Reading Materials
   B. AAA Auto Parts Co.
   C. ABCO Parts
   D. A Better Course for Test Preparation

7. Which of these files should appear between ABCO Parts and Aabar Books? 7.____
   A. A Bee C Reading Materials
   B. Abbey, Joanne
   C. Aabar Books
   D. A-Z Auto Parts

8. Which of these files should appear between Abbey, Joanne and Boman-Sylvan Law Firm? 8.____
   A. A Better Course for Test Preparation
   B. BMW Autowerks
   C. Chappell-Murray, Inc.
   D. Aabar Books

9. Which of these files should appear between Abbey, Joanne and C Q Service? 9.____
   A. A-Z Auto Parts, Inc.
   B. BMW Autowerks
   C. Choices A and B
   D. Chappell-Murray, Inc.

10. Which of these files should appear between C Q Service Company and Emcrisco? 10.____
    A. Chappell-Murray, Inc.
    B. E&E Life Insurance
    C. Gigi Arts
    D. Choices A and B

11. Which of these files should NOT appear between C Q Service Company and E&E Life Insurance? 11.____
    A. Gordon, Jon & Associates
    B. Emcrisco
    C. Gigi Arts
    D. All of the above

12. Which of these files should appear between Chappell-Murray, Inc. and   12.____
    Gigi Arts?
    A. C Q Service Inc., E&E Life Insurance, and Emcrisco
    B. Emcrisco, E&E Life Insurance, and Gordon, Jon & Associates
    C. E&E Life Insurance, and Emcrisco
    D. Emcrisco and Gordon, Jon & Associates

13. Which of these files should appear between Gordon, Jon & Associates and   13.____
    SOS Plumbing?
    A. Gigi Arts   B. Schmidt, J.B. Co.
    C. Choices A and B   D. None of the above

14. Each of the choices lists the four files in their proper alphabetical order   14.____
    EXCEPT
    A. E&E Life Insurance; Gigi Arts; Gordon, Jon & Associates; SOS Plumbing
    B. E&E Life Insurance; Emcrisco; Gigi Arts; SOS Plumbing
    C. Emcrisco; Gordon, Jon & Associates; SOS Plumbing; Schmidt, J.B. Co.
    D. Emcrisco; Gigi Arts; Gordon, Jon & Associates; SOS Plumbing

15. Which of the choices lists the four files in their proper alphabetical order?   15.____
    A. Gigi Arts; Gordon, Jon & Associates; SOS Plumbing; Schmidt, J.B. Co.
    B. Gordon, Jon & Associates; Gigi Arts; Schmidt, J.B. Co.; SOS Plumbing
    C. Gordon, Jon & Associates; Gigi Arts; SOS Plumbing; Schmidt, J.B. Co.
    D. Gigi Arts; Gordon, Jon & Associates; Schmidt, J.B. Co.; SOS Plumbing

16. The alphabetical filing order of two businesses with identical names is   16.____
    determined by the
    A. length of time each business has been operating
    B. addresses of the businesses
    C. last name of the company president
    D. no one of the above

17. In an alphabetical filing system, if a business name includes a number, it should   17.____
    be
    A. disregarded
    B. considered a number and placed at the end of an alphabetical section
    C. treated as though it were written in words and alphabetized accordingly
    D. considered a number and placed at the beginning of an alphabetical
       section

18. If a business name includes a contraction (such as *don't* or *it's*), how should   18.____
    that word be treated in an alphabetical system?
    A. Divide the word into its separate parts and treat it as two words
    B. Ignore the letters that come after the apostrophe
    C. Ignore the word that contains the contraction
    D. Ignore the apostrophe and consider all letters in the contraction

19. In what order should the parts of an address be considered when using an alphabetical filing system?   19._____
    A. City or town; state; street name; house or building number
    B. State; city or town; street name; house or building number
    C. House or building number; street name; city or town; state
    D. Street name; city or town; state

20. A business record should be cross-referenced when a(n)   20._____
    A. organization is known by an abbreviated name
    B. business has a name change because of a sale, incorporation, or other reason
    C. business is known by a *coined* or common name which differs from a dictionary spelling
    D. all of the above

21. A geographical filing system is MOST effective when   21._____
    A. location is more important than name
    B. many names or titles sound alike
    C. dealing with companies who have offices all over the world
    D. filing personal and business files

Questions 22-25.

DIRECTIONS: Questions 22 through 25 are to be answered on the basis of the list of items below, which are to be filed geographically. Organize the items geographically and then answer the questions.

   I. University Press at Berkeley, U.S.
   II. Maria Sanchez, Mexico City, Mexico
   III. Great Expectations Ltd. in London, England
   IV. Justice League, Cape Town, South Africa, Africa
   V. Crown Pearls Ltd. in London, England
   VI. Joseph Prasad in London, England

22. Which of the following arrangements of the items is composed according to the policy of: *Continent, Country, City, Firm or Individual Name?*   22._____
    A. V, III, IV, VI, II, I   B. IV, V, III, VI, II, I
    C. I, IV, V, III, VI, II   D. IV, V, III, VI, I, II

23. Which of the following files is arranged according to the policy of: 23._____
    Continent, Country, City, Firm or Individual Name?
    A. South Africa; Africa; Cape Town; Justice League
    B. Mexico; Mexico City; Maria Sanchez
    C. North America; United States; Berkeley; University Press
    D. England; Europe; London; Prasad, Joseph

5 (#1)

24. Which of the following arrangements of the items is composed according to the policy of: *Country, City, Firm or Individual Name*?   24.____
    A. V, VI, III, II, IV, I
    B. I, V, VI, III, II, IV
    C. VI, V, III, II, IV, I
    D. V, III, VI, II, IV, I

25. Which of the following files is arranged according to a policy of: *Country, City, Firm or Individual Name*?   25.____
    A. England; London; Crown Pearls Ltd.
    B. North America; United States; Berkeley; University Press
    C. Africa; Cape Town; Justice League
    D. Mexico City; Mexico; Maria Sanchez

26. Under which of the following circumstances would a phonetic filing system be MOST effective?   26.____
    A. When the person in charge of filing can't spell very well
    B. With large files with names that sound alike
    C. With large files with names that are spelled alike
    D. All of the above

Questions 27-29.

DIRECTIONS: Questions 27 through 29 are to be answered on the basis of the following list of numerical files.

    I.   391-023-100
    II. 361-132-170
    III. 385-732-200
    IV. 381-432-150
    V.   391-632-387
    VI. 361-423-303
    VII. 391-123-271

27. Which of the following arrangements of the files follows a consecutive-digit system?   27.____
    A. II, III, IV, I   B. I, V, VII, III   C. II, IV, III, I   D. III, I, V, VII

28. Which of the following arrangements follows a terminal-digit system?   28.____
    A. I, VII, II, IV, III
    B. II, I, IV, V, VII
    C. VII, VI, V, IV, III
    D. I, IV, II, III, VII

29. Which of the following lists follows a middle-digit system?   29.____
    A. I, VII, II, VI, IV, V, III
    B. I, II, VII, IV, VI, V, III
    C. VII, II, I, III, V, VI, IV
    D. VII, I, II, IV, VI, V, III

Questions 30-31.

DIRECTIONS: Questions 30 and 31 are to be answered on the basis of the following information.

  I. Reconfirm Laura Bates appointment with James Caldecort on December 12 at 9:30 A.M.
  II. Laurence Kinder contact Julia Lucas on August 3 and set up a meeting for week of September 23 at 4 P.M.
  III. John Lutz contact Larry Waverly on August 3 and set up appointment for September 23 at 9:30 A.M.
  IV. Call for tickets for Gerry Stanton August 21 for New Jersey on September 23, flight 143 at 4:43 P.M.

30. A chronological file for the above information would be 30._____
    A. IV, III, II, I   B. III, II, IV, I   C. IV, II, III, I   D. III, I, II, IV

31. Using the above information, a chronological file for the date September 23 would be 31._____
    A. II, III, IV   B. III, I, IV   C. III, II, IV   D. IV, III, II

Questions 32-34.

DIRECTIONS: Questions 32 through 34 are to be answered on the basis of the following information.

  I. Call Roger Epstein, Ashoke Naipaul, Jon Anderson, and Sara Washingon on April 19 at 1:00 P.M. to set up meeting with Alika D'Ornay for June 6 in New York.
  II. Call Martin Ames before noon on April 19 to confirm afternoon meeting with Bob Greenwood on April 20th.
  III. Set up meeting room at noon for 2:30 P.M. meeting on April 19th.
  IV. Ashley Stanton contact Bob Greenwood at 9:00 A.M. on April 20 and set up meeting for June 6 at 8:30 A.M.
  V. Carol Guiland contact Shelby Van Ness during afternoon of April 20 and set up meeting for June 6 at 10:00 A.M.
  VI. Call airline and reserve tickets on June 6 for Roger Epstein trip to Denver on July 8.
  VII. Meeting at 2:30 P.M. on April 19th.

32. A chronological file for all of the above information would be 32._____
    A. II, I, III, VII, V, IV, VI   B. III, VII, II, I, IV, V, VI
    C. III, VII, I, II, V, IV, VI   D. II, III, I, VII, IV, V, VI

33. A chronological file for the date of April 19th would be 33._____
    A. II, III, VII, I   B. II, III, I, VII   C. VII, I, III, II   D. III, VII, I, II

34. Add the following information to the file, and then create a chronological file 34._____
for April 20th: VIII. April 20: 3:00 P.M. meeting between Bob Greenwood and
Martin Ames.
    A. IV, V, VIII   B. IV, VIII, V   C. VIII, V, IV   D. V, IV, VIII

35. The PRIMARY advantage of computer records over a manual system is 35._____
    A. speed of retrieval   B. accuracy
    C. cost   D. potential file loss

KEY (CORRECT ANSWERS)

1. B	11. D	21. A	31. C
2. C	12. C	22. B	32. D
3. D	13. B	23. C	33. B
4. A	14. C	24. D	34. A
5. D	15. D	25. A	35. A
6. C	16. B	26. B	
7. B	17. C	27. C	
8. B	18. D	28. D	
9. C	19. A	29. A	
10. D	20. D	30. B	

WORD MEANING COMMENTARY

DESCRIPTION OF THE TEST
On many examinations, you will have questions about the meaning of words or vocabulary.

In this type of question, you have to state what a word or phrase means. (A phrase is a group of words.) This word or phrase is in capital letters in a sentence. You are also given for each question five other words or groups of words—lettered A, B, C, D, and E—as possible answers. One of these words or groups of words means the same as the word or group of words in CAPITAL letters. Only one is right. You are to pick out the one that is right and select the letter of your answer.

HINTS FOR ANSWERING WORD-MEANING QUESTIONS
Read each question carefully.

Choose the best answer of the five choices even though it is not the word you might use yourself.

Answer first those that you know. Then do the others.

If you know that some of the suggested answers are not right, pay no more attention to them.

Be sure that you have selected an answer for every question, even if you have to guess.

SAMPLE QUESTIONS

DIRECTIONS: For the following questions, select the word or group of words lettered A, B, C, D, or E that means MOST NEARLY the same as the word in capital letters. Indicate the letter of the CORRECT answer for each question.

SAMPLE QUESTIONS 1 AND 2

1. The letter was SHORT. SHORT means MOST NEARLY
   A. tall   B. wide   C. brief   D. heavy   E. dark

EXPLANATION
SHORT is a word you have used to describe something that is small, or not long, or little, etc. Therefore, you would not have to spend much time figuring out the right answer. You would choose C. brief.

2. The young man is VIGOROUS. VIGOROUS means MOST NEARLY
   A. serious   B. reliable   C. courageous
   D. strong   E. talented

EXPLANATION
VIGOROUS is a word that you have probably used yourself or read somewhere. It carries with it the idea of being active, full of pep, etc. Which one of the five choices comes closest to meaning that? Certainly not A. serious, B. reliable, or E. talented; C. courageous—maybe, D. strong—maybe. But between courageous or strong, you would have to agree that strong is the better choice. Therefore, you would choose D.

WORD MEANING

EXAMINATION SECTION

TEST 1

DIRECTIONS: For the following questions, select the word or group of words lettered A, B, C, D, or E that means MOST NEARLY the same as the word in capital letters. *PRINT THE LETTER OF THE CORRECT ANSWER IN THE SPACE AT THE RIGHT.*

1. To SULK means MOST NEARLY to 1.____
   A. cry   B. annoy   C. lament   D. be sullen   E. scorn

2. To FLOUNDER means MOST NEARLY to 2.____
   A. investigate   B. label   C. struggle
   D. consent   E. escape

3. PARLEY means MOST NEARLY 3.____
   A. discussion   B. thoroughfare   C. salon
   D. surrender   E. division

4. MAESTRO means MOST NEARLY 4.____
   A. official   B. ancestor   C. teacher
   D. watchman   E. alien

5. MEANDERING means MOST NEARLY 5.____
   A. cruel   B. adjusting   C. winding
   D. smooth   E. combining

6. GNARLED means MOST NEARLY 6.____
   A. angry   B. bitter   C. twisted
   D. ancient   E. embroidered

7. TEMPERANCE means MOST NEARLY 7.____
   A. moderation   B. climate   C. carelessness
   D. disagreeableness   E. rigidity

8. A PRECARIOUS position is one that is 8.____
   A. foresighted   B. careful   C. modest
   D. headstrong   E. uncertain

9. COVETOUS means MOST NEARLY 9.____
   A. undisciplined   B. grasping   C. timid
   D. insincere   E. secretive

10. PRIVATION means MOST NEARLY 10.____
    A. reward   B. superiority in rank
    C. hardship   D. suitability of behavior
    E. solitude

TEST 2

DIRECTIONS: For the following questions, select the word or group of words lettered A, B, C, D, or E that means MOST NEARLY the same as the word in capital letters. *PRINT THE LETTER OF THE CORRECT ANSWER IN THE SPACE AT THE RIGHT.*

1. To INFILTRATE means MOST NEARLY to
   A. pass through
   B. stop
   C. consider
   D. challenge openly
   E. meet secretly

   1.____

2. REVOCATION means MOST NEARLY
   A. certificate
   B. repeal
   C. animation
   D. license
   E. plea

   2.____

3. LOQUACIOUS means MOST NEARLY
   A. grim
   B. stern
   C. talkative
   D. lighthearted
   E. liberty-loving

   3.____

4. APERTURE means MOST NEARLY
   A. basement
   B. opening
   C. phantom
   D. protective coloring
   E. light refreshment

   4.____

5. A PUNGENT odor is one that is
   A. biting
   B. smooth
   C. quarrelsome
   D. wrong
   E. proud

   5.____

6. To CORROBORATE means MOST NEARLY to
   A. deny
   B. elaborate
   C. confirm
   D. gnaw
   E. state

   6.____

7. BENEVOLENCE means MOST NEARLY
   A. good fortune
   B. well-being
   C. inheritance
   D. violence
   E. charitableness

   7.____

8. PETULANT means MOST NEARLY
   A. rotten
   B. fretful
   C. unrelated
   D. weird
   E. throbbing

   8.____

9. DERELICT means MOST NEARLY
   A. abandoned
   B. widowed
   C. faithful
   D. insincere
   E. hysterical

   9.____

10. INCISIVE means MOST NEARLY
    A. stimulating
    B. accidental
    C. brief
    D. penetrating
    E. final

    10.____

TEST 3

DIRECTIONS: For the following questions, select the word or group of words lettered A, B, C, D, or E that means MOST NEARLY the same as the word in capital letters. *PRINT THE LETTER OF THE CORRECT ANSWER IN THE SPACE AT THE RIGHT.*

1. To LAUD means MOST NEARLY to
   A. praise B. cleanse C. replace
   D. squander E. frown upon

   1.____

2. To TAUNT means MOST NEARLY to
   A. jeer at B. tighten C. rescue
   D. interest E. ward off

   2.____

3. DEITY means MOST NEARLY
   A. renown B. divinity C. delicacy
   D. destiny E. futility

   3.____

4. GRAVITY means MOST NEARLY
   A. displeasure B. thankfulness C. suffering
   D. roughness E. seriousness

   4.____

5. A CONTEMPTUOUS author is one that is
   A. thoughtful B. soiled C. dishonorable
   D. scornful E. self-satisfied

   5.____

6. To WAIVE means MOST NEARLY to
   A. exercise B. swing C. claim
   D. give up E. wear out

   6.____

7. To ASPIRE means MOST NEARLY to
   A. fade away B. excite C. desire earnestly
   D. breathe heavily E. roughen

   7.____

8. PERTINENT means MOST NEARLY
   A. related B. saucy C. quick
   D. impatient E. excited

   8.____

9. DEVASTATION means MOST NEARLY
   A. desolation B. displeasure C. dishonor
   D. neglect E. religious fervor

   9.____

10. IMMINENT means MOST NEARLY
    A. sudden B. important C. delayed
    D. threatening E. forceful

    10.____

TEST 4

DIRECTIONS: For the following questions, select the word or group of words lettered A, B, C, D, or E that means MOST NEARLY the same as the word in capital letters. *PRINT THE LETTER OF THE CORRECT ANSWER IN THE SPACE AT THE RIGHT.*

1. CONTROVERSAL means MOST NEARLY
   A. faultfinding   B. pleasant   C. debatable
   D. ugly   E. talkative

   1.____

2. GHASTLY means MOST NEARLY
   A. hasty   B. furious   C. breathless
   D. deathlike   E. spiritual

   2.____

3. A BELLIGERENT attitude is one that is
   A. worldly   B. warlike   C. loudmouthed
   D. furious   E. artistic

   3.____

4. PROFICIENCY means MOST NEARLY
   A. wisdom   B. oversupply   C. expertness
   D. advancement   E. sincerity

   4.____

5. COMPASSION means MOST NEARLY
   A. rage   B. strength of character
   C. forcefulness   D. sympathy
   E. uniformity

   5.____

6. DISSENSION means MOST NEARLY
   A. treatise   B. pretense   C. fear
   D. lineage   E. discord

   6.____

7. To INTIMATE means MOST NEARLY to
   A. charm   B. hint   C. disguise
   D. frighten   E. hum

   7.____

8. To BERATE means MOST NEARLY to
   A. classify   B. scold   C. underestimate
   D. take one's time   E. evaluate

   8.____

9. DEARTH means MOST NEARLY
   A. scarcity   B. width   C. affection
   D. wealth   E. warmth

   9.____

10. To MEDITATE means MOST NEARLY to
    A. rest   B. stare   C. doze
    D. make peace   E. reflect

    10.____

TEST 5

DIRECTIONS: For the following questions, select the word or group of words lettered A, B, C, D, or E that means MOST NEARLY the same as the word in capital letters. *PRINT THE LETTER OF THE CORRECT ANSWER IN THE SPACE AT THE RIGHT.*

1. BONDAGE means MOST NEARLY
   A. poverty
   B. redemption
   C. slavery
   D. retirement
   E. complaint

   1._____

2. AGILITY means MOST NEARLY
   A. wisdom
   B. nimbleness
   C. agreeable
   D. simplicity
   E. excitement

   2._____

3. To ABDICATE means MOST NEARLY to
   A. achieve
   B. protest
   C. renounce
   D. demand
   E. steal

   3._____

4. To STIFLE means MOST NEARLY to
   A. talk nonsense
   B. sidestep
   C. depress
   D. smother
   E. stick

   4._____

5. EDICT means MOST NEARLY
   A. abbreviation
   B. lie
   C. carbon copy
   D. correction
   E. decree

   5._____

6. AMITY means MOST NEARLY
   A. ill will
   B. hope
   C. pity
   D. friendship
   E. pleasure

   6._____

7. COERCION means MOST NEARLY
   A. force
   B. disgust
   C. suspicion
   D. pleasure
   E. criticism

   7._____

8. To ABASH means MOST NEARLY to
   A. embarrass
   B. encourage
   C. punish
   D. surrender
   E. overthrow

   8._____

9. TACITURN means MOST NEARLY
   A. weak
   B. evil
   C. tender
   D. silent
   E. sensitive

   9._____

10. REMISS means MOST NEARLY
    A. memorable
    B. neglectful
    C. useless
    D. prompt
    E. exact

    10._____

TEST 6

DIRECTIONS: For the following questions, select the word or group of words lettered A, B, C, D, or E that means MOST NEARLY the same as the word in capital letters. *PRINT THE LETTER OF THE CORRECT ANSWER IN THE SPACE AT THE RIGHT.*

1. STAGNANT means MOST NEARLY
   A. inactive
   B. alert
   C. selfish
   D. difficult
   E. scornful

   1.____

2. MANDATORY means MOST NEARLY
   A. instant
   B. obligatory
   C. evident
   D. strategic
   E. unequaled

   2.____

3. INFERNAL means MOST NEARLY
   A. immodest
   B. incomplete
   C. domestic
   D. second-rate
   E. fiendish

   3.____

4. To EXONERATE means MOST NEARLY to
   A. free from blame
   B. warn
   C. drive out
   D. overcharge
   E. plead

   4.____

5. ARBITER means MOST NEARLY
   A. friend
   B. judge
   C. drug
   D. tree surgeon
   E. truant

   5.____

6. ENMITY means MOST NEARLY
   A. boredom
   B. puzzle
   C. ill will
   D. offensive language
   E. entanglement

   6.____

7. To DISCRIMINATE means MOST NEARLY to
   A. fail
   B. delay
   C. accuses
   D. distinguish
   E. reject

   7.____

8. DERISION means MOST NEARLY
   A. disgust
   B. ridicule
   C. fear
   D. anger
   E. heredity

   8.____

9. EXULTANT means MOST NEARLY
   A. essential
   B. elated
   C. praiseworthy
   D. plentiful
   E. high-priced

   9.____

10. OSTENSIBLE
    A. vibrating
    B. odd
    C. apparent
    D. standard
    E. ornate

    10.____

TEST 7

DIRECTIONS: For the following questions, select the word or group of words lettered A, B, C, D, or E that means MOST NEARLY the same as the word in capital letters. *PRINT THE LETTER OF THE CORRECT ANSWER IN THE SPACE AT THE RIGHT.*

1. To ABHOR means MOST NEARLY
   A. hate
   B. admire
   C. taste
   D. skip
   E. resign

2. DUTIFUL means MOST NEARLY
   A. lasting
   B. sluggish
   C. required
   D. soothing
   E. obedient

3. ZEALOT means MOST NEARLY
   A. breeze
   B. enthusiast
   C. vault
   D. wild animal
   E. musical instrument

4. A MAGNANIMOUS attitude is one that is
   A. high-minded
   B. faithful
   C. concerned
   D. individual
   E. small

5. To CITE means MOST NEARLY to
   A. protest
   B. depart
   C. quote
   D. agitate
   E. perform

6. OBLIVION means MOST NEARLY
   A. hindrance
   B. accident
   C. courtesy
   D. forgetfulness
   E. old age

7. CARDINAL means MOST NEARLY
   A. independent
   B. well-organized
   C. subordinate
   D. dignified
   E. chief

8. To DEPLETE means MOST NEARLY to
   A. restrain
   B. corrupt
   C. despair
   D. exhaust
   E. spread out

9. To SUPERSEDE means MOST NEARLY to
   A. retire
   B. replace
   C. overflow
   D. bless
   E. oversee

10. SPORADIC means MOST NEARLY
    A. bad-tempered
    B. infrequent
    C. radical
    D. reckless
    E. humble

TEST 8

DIRECTIONS: For the following questions, select the word or group of words lettered A, B, C, D, or E that means MOST NEARLY the same as the word in capital letters. *PRINT THE LETTER OF THE CORRECT ANSWER IN THE SPACE AT THE RIGHT.*

1. To NEUTRALIZE means MOST NEARLY to
   - A. entangle
   - B. strengthen
   - C. counteract
   - D. combat
   - E. converse

   1.____

2. To INSINUATE means MOST NEARLY to
   - A. destroy
   - B. hint
   - C. do wrong
   - D. accuse
   - E. release

   2.____

3. DIMINUTIVE means MOST NEARLY
   - A. proud
   - B. slow
   - C. small
   - D. watery
   - E. puzzling

   3.____

4. PLIGHT means MOST NEARLY
   - A. departure
   - B. weight
   - C. conspiracy
   - D. predicament
   - E. stamp

   4.____

5. An ILLICIT relationship is one that is
   - A. unlawful
   - B. overpowering
   - C. ill-advised
   - D. small-scale
   - E. unreadable

   5.____

6. A BENIGN manner is one that is
   - A. contagious
   - B. fatal
   - C. ignorant
   - D. kindly
   - E. decorative

   6.____

7. REVERIE means MOST NEARLY
   - A. abusive language
   - B. love song
   - C. backward step
   - D. daydream
   - E. holy man

   7.____

8. APPREHENSIVE means MOST NEARLY
   - A. quiet
   - B. firm
   - C. curious
   - D. sincere
   - E. fearful

   8.____

9. To RECOIL means MOST NEARLY to
   - A. shrink
   - B. attract
   - C. electrify
   - D. adjust
   - E. fear

   9.____

10. GUISE means MOST NEARLY
    - A. trickery
    - B. request
    - C. innocence
    - D. misdeed
    - E. appearance

    10.____

TEST 9

DIRECTIONS: For the following questions, select the word or group of words lettered A, B, C, D, or E that means MOST NEARLY the same as the word in capital letters. *PRINT THE LETTER OF THE CORRECT ANSWER IN THE SPACE AT THE RIGHT.*

1. To RELINQUISH means MOST NEARLY to
   A. regret
   B. abandon
   C. pursue
   D. secure
   E. penetrate

   1.____

2. INJUNCTION means MOST NEARLY
   A. error
   B. attack
   C. injustice
   D. suggestion
   E. order

   2.____

3. ADVENT means MOST NEARLY
   A. attachment
   B. reference
   C. arrival
   D. excitement
   E. vent

   3.____

4. BICAMERAL means MOST NEARLY
   A. dealing with life forms
   B. meeting on alternate years
   C. over-sweet
   D. having two legislative branches
   E. having two meanings

   4.____

5. A PERVERSE attitude is one that is
   A. contrary
   B. stingy
   C. unfortunate
   D. hereditary
   E. easygoing

   5.____

6. To THWART means MOST NEARLY to
   A. assist
   B. whimper
   C. slice
   D. escape
   E. block

   6.____

7. DEVOID means MOST NEARLY
   A. empty
   B. illegal
   C. affectionate
   D. pious
   E. annoying

   7.____

8. A BLAND manner is one that is
   A. gentle
   B. guilty
   C. salty
   D. unfinished
   E. majestic

   8.____

9. To OSTRACIZE means MOST NEARLY to
   A. flatter
   B. scold
   C. show off
   D. banish
   E. vibrate

   9.____

10. CANDOR means MOST NEARLY
    A. sociability
    B. outspokenness
    C. grief
    D. light
    E. flattery

    10.____

TEST 10

DIRECTIONS: For the following questions, select the word or group of words lettered A, B, C, D, or E that means MOST NEARLY the same as the word in capital letters. *PRINT THE LETTER OF THE CORRECT ANSWER IN THE SPACE AT THE RIGHT.*

1. ACQUIT means MOST NEARLY
   A. increase B. harden C. clear
   D. sharpen E. sentence

2. DEXTERITY means MOST NEARLY
   A. conceit B. skill C. insistence
   D. embarrassment E. guidance

3. ASSIMILATE means MOST NEARLY
   A. absorb B. imitate C. maintain
   D. outrun E. curb

4. DESPONDENCY means MOST NEARLY
   A. relief B. gratitude C. dejection
   D. hatred E. poverty

5. A BUOYANT manner is one that is
   A. conceited B. cautioning C. youthful
   D. musical E. cheerful

6. CULINARY means MOST NEARLY
   A. having to do with cooking B. pertaining to dressmaking
   C. fond of eating D. loving money
   E. tending to be secretive

7. CAPRICE means MOST NEARLY
   A. wisdom B. ornament C. pillar
   D. whim E. energy

8. DETERRENT means MOST NEARLY
   A. restraining B. cleansing C. deciding
   D. concluding E. crumbling

9. A PUGNACIOUS attitude is one that is
   A. sticky B. cowardly C. precise
   D. vigorous E. quarrelsome

10. ABSCOND means MOST NEARLY
    A. detest B. reduce C. swallow up
    D. dismiss E. flee

TEST 11

DIRECTIONS: For the following questions, select the word or group of words lettered A, B, C, D, or E that means MOST NEARLY the same as the word in capital letters. *PRINT THE LETTER OF THE CORRECT ANSWER IN THE SPACE AT THE RIGHT.*

1. DOLDRUMS means MOST NEARLY
   - A. delirium
   - B. rage
   - C. saturation
   - D. incarceration
   - E. listlessness

   1.____

2. DOUR means MOST NEARLY
   - A. gloomy
   - B. cowardly
   - C. untidy
   - D. stingy
   - E. doubtful

   2.____

3. DRAGOON means MOST NEARLY
   - A. defy
   - B. enlist
   - C. surrender
   - D. lead
   - E. persecute

   3.____

4. EMPIRICAL means MOST NEARLY
   - A. experiential
   - B. undeniable
   - C. melancholy
   - D. territorial
   - E. traditional

   4.____

5. ENCOMIUM means MOST NEARLY
   - A. antidote
   - B. adage
   - C. anteroom
   - D. eulogy
   - E. bombast

   5.____

6. ENTOMOLOGIST means MOST NEARLY student of
   - A. insects
   - B. fish
   - C. words
   - D. fossils
   - E. reptiles

   6.____

7. EPHEMERAL means MOST NEARLY
   - A. persistent
   - B. useless
   - C. effete
   - D. visionary
   - E. short-lived

   7.____

8. ETIOLOGY means MOST NEARLY
   - A. epitome
   - B. inertia
   - C. astronomy
   - D. disease
   - E. cause

   8.____

9. FETISH means MOST NEARLY
   - A. tuft of hair above horse's foot
   - B. embryo of an animal
   - C. object of excessive devotion
   - D. spirit of a festival
   - E. feast of the Haitians

   9.____

10. GAMUT means MOST NEARLY
    - A. gamble
    - B. alphabet
    - C. keys
    - D. chess move
    - E. range

    10.____

TEST 12

DIRECTIONS: For the following questions, select the word or group of words lettered A, B, C, D, or E that means MOST NEARLY the same as the word in capital letters. *PRINT THE LETTER OF THE CORRECT ANSWER IN THE SPACE AT THE RIGHT.*

1. HALLOW means MOST NEARLY
   A. shout aloud
   B. make sacred
   C. haunt
   D. reveal
   E. hole out

2. HEGEMONY means MOST NEARLY
   A. flight
   B. restraint
   C. nationalism
   D. autonomy
   E. leadership

3. HERMETIC means MOST NEARLY
   A. air-tight
   B. protruding
   C. sequestered
   D. briskly
   E. ascetic

4. IBID means MOST NEARLY
   A. that is
   B. as an example
   C. the same
   D. see above
   E. and so forth

5. IMPUGN means MOST NEARLY
   A. enhance
   B. attribute
   C. assail
   D. compromise
   E. defend

6. INCIPIENT means MOST NEARLY
   A. tasteless
   B. annoying
   C. unyielding
   D. ultimate
   E. commencing

7. INEXORABLE means MOST NEARLY
   A. hateful
   B. conciliatory
   C. unresponsive
   D. relentless
   E. pliant

8. INTREPID means MOST NEARLY
   A. awesome
   B. bellicose
   C. undisciplined
   D. courageous
   E. pacific

9. INVECTIVE means MOST NEARLY
   A. self study
   B. geometrical analysis
   C. verbal abuse
   D. hard-won victory
   E. indecision

10. INVEIGLED means MOST NEARLY
    A. ensnared
    B. terrified
    C. coerced
    D. corrupted
    E. incarcerated

TEST 13

DIRECTIONS: For the following questions, select the word or group of words lettered A, B, C, D, or E that means MOST NEARLY the same as the word in capital letters. *PRINT THE LETTER OF THE CORRECT ANSWER IN THE SPACE AT THE RIGHT.*

1. ITERANT means MOST NEARLY 1.____
   - A. distant
   - B. repeating
   - C. directed
   - D. wandering
   - E. errant

2. LAMPOON means MOST NEARLY 2.____
   - A. magazine
   - B. satire
   - C. clown
   - D. lament
   - E. shade

3. LAPIDARY means MOST NEARLY one who 3.____
   - A. collects butterflies
   - B. breaks up large estates
   - C. indulges the senses
   - D. judges the quality of beverages
   - E. cuts precious stones

4. MERETRICIOUS means MOST NEARLY 4.____
   - A. according to the metric system
   - B. deserving
   - C. scholarly
   - D. indigent
   - E. tawdry

5. MITIGATE means MOST NEARLY 5.____
   - A. exonerate
   - B. handicap
   - C. aggravate
   - D. appease
   - E. defile

6. MORES means MOST NEARLY 6.____
   - A. beginnings
   - B. conglomerations
   - C. curses
   - D. mutations
   - E. customs

7. NOSTRUM means MOST NEARLY 7.____
   - A. ocean sea
   - B. paternity
   - C. remedy
   - D. pungency
   - E. family

8. OBJURGATE means MOST NEARLY 8.____
   - A. chide
   - B. sacrifice
   - C. oppose
   - D. purge
   - E. repeat

9. OSSIFY means MOST NEARLY 9.____
   - A. vacillate
   - B. harden
   - C. categorize
   - D. tipple
   - E. abstain

10. PARLOUS means MOST NEARLY 10.____
    - A. wise
    - B. bargaining
    - C. talkative
    - D. dangerous
    - E. partial

TEST 14

DIRECTIONS: For the following questions, select the word or group of words lettered A, B, C, D, or E that means MOST NEARLY the same as the word in capital letters. *PRINT THE LETTER OF THE CORRECT ANSWER IN THE SPACE AT THE RIGHT.*

1. ADVENTITIOUS means MOST NEARLY
   - A. opportunistic
   - B. daring
   - C. helpful
   - D. deceptive
   - E. extrinsic

2. AMBIVALENT means MOST NEARLY
   - A. helpful in walking
   - B. equally skillful with both hands
   - C. simultaneously hating and loving
   - D. ambiguous in origin
   - E. equivalent

3. AMORPHOUS means MOST NEARLY
   - A. inelegant
   - B. clamorous
   - C. quiescent
   - D. ardent
   - E. formless

4. ANATHEMA means MOST NEARLY
   - A. despair
   - B. benevolence
   - C. disputation
   - D. anomaly
   - E. curse

5. APIARY means MOST NEARLY
   - A. bee house
   - B. pear-shaped figure
   - C. main-traveled road
   - D. monkey cage
   - E. bird house

6. APORYPHAL means MOST NEARLY of
   - A. scholarly pursuits
   - B. sacred origin
   - C. ancient beginnings
   - D. ecclesiastical power
   - E. doubtful authenticity

7. APOSTASY means MOST NEARLY
   - A. confirmation
   - B. detection
   - C. supposition
   - D. canonization
   - E. deification

8. ASCETIC means MOST NEARLY
   - A. exclusive
   - B. sharp
   - C. fragrant
   - D. austere
   - E. authentic

9. BADINAGE means MOST NEARLY
   - A. indifference
   - B. song
   - C. banter
   - D. mucilage
   - E. autarchy

10. BOGGLE means MOST NEARLY
    - A. dampen
    - B. hesitate
    - C. undermine
    - D. disarrange
    - E. haggle

TEST 15

DIRECTIONS: For the following questions, select the word or group of words lettered A, B, C, D, or E that means MOST NEARLY the same as the word in capital letters. *PRINT THE LETTER OF THE CORRECT ANSWER IN THE SPACE AT THE RIGHT.*

1. BUCOLIC means MOST NEARLY
   A. rustic
   B. flatulent
   C. angry
   D. loud
   E. bureaucratic

2. CAESURA means MOST NEARLY
   A. genesis
   B. referring to Caesar
   C. tyranny
   D. domain
   E. break

3. CAREEN means MOST NEARLY
   A. lurch
   B. wail
   C. pour
   D. contain
   E. corrode

4. CARET means MOST NEARLY
   A. measure of weight
   B. sign of omission
   C. technique in ballet
   D. growth of root
   E. notice for caution

5. CARIES means MOST NEARLY
   A. treatment
   B. convalescent
   C. decay
   D. chemicals
   E. roots

6. CASIOST means MOST NEARLY
   A. sophistical reasoner
   B. careless worker
   C. innocent victim
   D. habitual late-comer
   E. frenzied lawyer

7. CHIMERICAL means MOST NEARLY
   A. scientific
   B. debasing
   C. well-ordered
   D. maniacal
   E. fanciful

8. CLABBER means MOST NEARLY
   A. gossip
   B. climb
   C. crop
   D. entwine
   E. curdle

9. COMME IL FAUT means MOST NEARLY
   A. unnecessary
   B. erroneous
   C. proper
   D. mixed
   E. illegal

10. CRYPTIC means MOST NEARLY
    A. succinct
    B. astringent
    C. death-like
    D. crotchety
    E. occult

TEST 16

DIRECTIONS: For the following questions, select the word or group of words lettered A, B, C, D, or E that means MOST NEARLY the same as the word in capital letters. *PRINT THE LETTER OF THE CORRECT ANSWER IN THE SPACE AT THE RIGHT.*

1. CYNOSURE means MOST NEARLY
   A. act of completion   B. occupation of ease   C. attitude of doubt
   D. center of attraction   E. cynical statement

   1.____

2. DEBENTURE means MOST NEARLY
   A. written acknowledgment of debt   B. sale of preferred stock
   C. illegal sale of securities   D. dividend on stocks or bonds
   E. disclaimer in a prospectus

   2.____

3. DEMURRER means MOST NEARLY
   A. promotion   B. objection   C. interrogation
   D. retainer   E. demerit

   3.____

4. DERELICTION means MOST NEARLY
   A. general decline   B. damaging criticism   C. probable cause
   D. abandoned vessel   E. failure in duty

   4.____

5. DESCRIED means MOST NEARLY
   A. delimned   B. defined   C. rejected
   D. erred   E. discerned

   5.____

6. DESIDERATUM means MOST NEARLY
   A. final outcome   B. hearty approval   C. last remnant
   D. desired object   E. prescribed treatment

   6.____

7. DISCRETE means MOST NEARLY
   A. separate   B. reserved   C. foresighted
   D. unbounded   E. tactful

   7.____

8. DISINGENUOUS means MOST NEARLY
   A. unsophisticated   B. skillful   C. apathetic
   D. naïve   E. insincere

   8.____

9. DISSIDENT means MOST NEARLY
   A. malodorous   B. amoral   C. discordant
   D. unfeeling   E. divisive

   9.____

10. EGREGIOUS means MOST NEARLY
    A. debased   B. inconsequential   C. incorrigible
    D. egotistical   E. prominent

    10.____

TEST 17

DIRECTIONS: For the following questions, select the word or group of words lettered A, B, C, D, or E that means MOST NEARLY the same as the word in capital letters. *PRINT THE LETTER OF THE CORRECT ANSWER IN THE SPACE AT THE RIGHT.*

1. EMPATHY means MOST NEARLY
   - A. comatose condition
   - B. sympathetic understanding
   - C. depressed feeling
   - D. political subdivision
   - E. patriotic devotion

   1._____

2. ESOTERIC means MOST NEARLY
   - A. abstruse
   - B. intestinal
   - C. lively
   - D. joining
   - E. essential

   2._____

3. ESPERANTO means MOST NEARLY
   - A. fabled country
   - B. artificial language
   - C. European peace manifesto
   - D. place of abandoned hope
   - E. pertaining to the Elysian Fields

   3._____

4. EUPHEMISM means MOST NEARLY
   - A. pleasant sight
   - B. right direction
   - C. verbal platitude
   - D. buoyant feeling
   - E. inoffensive expression

   4._____

5. FINICAL means MOST NEARLY
   - A. blundering
   - B. fastidious
   - C. conclusive
   - D. maniacal
   - E. extravagant

   5._____

6. GUERDON means MOST NEARLY
   - A. debacle
   - B. shield
   - C. fruit
   - D. obstacle
   - E. recompense

   6._____

7. GYVES means MOST NEARLY
   - A. gallows
   - B. chains
   - C. barbs
   - D. vegetables
   - E. jives

   7._____

8. HEDONIST means MOST NEARLY
   - A. reviler
   - B. recluse
   - C. pleasure-seeker
   - D. savage
   - E. hermit

   8._____

9. HIATUS means MOST NEARLY
   - A. flower
   - B. gap
   - C. mistake
   - D. digression
   - E. hearsay

   9._____

10. IMBROGLIO means MOST NEARLY
    - A. secluded dwelling
    - B. impassioned plea
    - C. rampant destruction
    - D. petit point
    - E. complicated situation

    10._____

TEST 18

DIRECTIONS: For the following questions, select the word or group of words lettered A, B, C, D, or E that means MOST NEARLY the same as the word in capital letters. *PRINT THE LETTER OF THE CORRECT ANSWER IN THE SPACE AT THE RIGHT.*

1. IMPALPABLE means MOST NEARLY not
   A. truthful
   B. concrete
   C. throbbing
   D. deviating
   E. suggestive

   1.____

2. IMPECUNIOUS means MOST NEARLY
   A. poor
   B. wayward
   C. troublesome
   D. inordinate
   E. ingenuous

   2.____

3. IMPORTUNATE means MOST NEARLY
   A. critical
   B. empty-handed
   C. disastrous
   D. pusillanimous
   E. pressing

   3.____

4. IMPRIMIS means MOST NEARLY
   A. church dignitary
   B. sanction
   C. manuscript
   D. sacred song
   E. in the first place

   4.____

5. INURED means MOST NEARLY
   A. belligerent
   B. hardened
   C. apprehensive
   D. irreverent
   E. injured

   5.____

6. INVIDIOUS means MOST NEARLY
   A. obscure
   B. unconquerable
   C. offensive
   D. niggardly
   E. invariable

   6.____

7. JOCOSE means MOST NEARLY
   A. intemperate
   B. contemptuous
   C. morose
   D. nugatory
   E. facetious

   7.____

8. LACHRYMOSE means MOST NEARLY
   A. milky
   B. disdainful
   C. comic
   D. tearful
   E. comatose

   8.____

9. LISSOME means MOST NEARLY
   A. nimble
   B. comely
   C. laughable
   D. lackadaisical
   E. aggressive

   9.____

10. MERCURIAL means MOST NEARLY
    A. thermal
    B. coy
    C. volatile
    D. ponderous
    E. unchangeable

    10.____

KEYS (CORRECT ANSWERS)

TEST 1		TEST 2		TEST 3	
1. D	6. C	1. A	6. C	1. A	6. D
2. C	7. A	2. B	7. E	2. A	7. C
3. A	8. E	3. C	8. B	3. B	8. A
4. C	9. B	4. B	9. A	4. E	9. A
5. C	10. C	5. A	10. D	5. D	10. D

TEST 4		TEST 5		TEST 6	
1. C	6. E	1. C	6. D	1. A	6. D
2. D	7. B	2. B	7. A	2. B	7. D
3. B	8. B	3. C	8. A	3. E	8. B
4. C	9. A	4. D	9. D	4. A	9. B
5. D	10. E	5. E	10. B	5. B	10. C

TEST 7		TEST 8		TEST 9	
1. A	6. D	1. C	6. D	1. B	6. E
2. E	7. E	2. B	7. D	2. E	7. A
3. B	8. D	3. C	8. E	3. C	8. A
4. A	9. B	4. D	9. A	4. D	9. D
5. C	10. B	5. A	10. E	5. A	10. B

TEST 10		TEST 11		TEST 12	
1. C	6. A	1. E	6. A	1. B	6. E
2. B	7. D	2. A	7. E	2. E	7. D
3. A	8. A	3. E	8. E	3. A	8. D
4. C	9. E	4. A	9. C	4. C	9. C
5. E	10. E	5. D	10. E	5. C	10. A

TEST 13		TEST 14		TEST 15	
1. B	6. E	1. E	6. E	1. A	6. A
2. B	7. C	2. C	7. B	2. E	7. E
3. E	8. A	3. E	8. D	3. A	8. E
4. E	9. B	4. E	9. C	4. B	9. C
5. D	10. D	5. A	10. B	5. C	10. E

TEST 16		TEST 17		TEST 18	
1. D	6. D	1. B	6. E	1. B	6. C
2. A	7. A	2. A	7. B	2. A	7. E
3. B	8. E	3. B	8. C	3. E	8. D
4. E	9. C	4. E	9. B	4. E	9. A
5. E	10. E	5. B	10. E	5. B	10. C

EXAMINATION SECTION
TEST 1

DIRECTIONS: In each of the following tests in this part, select the letter of the one MIS-SPELLED word in each of the following groups of words. If no word is misspelled, select the last item, letter E (none misspelled). *PRINT THE LETTER OF THE CORRECT ANSWER IN THE SPACE AT THE RIGHT.*

1. A. grateful   B. fundimental   C. census   1.____
   D. analysis   E. NONE MISSPELLED

2. A. installment   B. retrieve   C. concede   2.____
   D. dissapear   E. NONE MISSPELLED

3. A. accidentaly   B. dismissal   C. conscientious   3.____
   D. indelible   E. NONE MISSPELLED

4. A. perceive   B. carreer   C. anticipate   4.____
   D. acquire   E. NONE MISSPELLED

5. A. facility   B. reimburse   C. assortment   5.____
   D. guidance   E. NONE MISSPELLED

6. A. plentiful   B. across   C. advantagous   6.____
   D. similar   E. NONE MISSPELLED

7. A. omission   B. pamphlet   C. guarrantee   7.____
   D. repel   E. NONE MISSPELLED

8. A. maintenance   B. always   C. liable   8.____
   D. anouncement   E. NONE MISSPELLED

9. A. exaggerate   B. sieze   C. condemn   9.____
   D. commit   E. NONE MISSPELLED

10. A. pospone   B. altogether   C. grievance   10.____
    D. excessive   E. NONE MISSPELLED

11. A. arguing   B. correspondance   C. forfeit   11.____
    D. dissension   E. NONE MISSPELLED

12. A. occasion   B. description   C. prejudice   12.____
    D. elegible   E. NONE MISSPELLED

13. A. accomodate   B. initiative   C. changeable   13.____
    D. enroll   E. NONE MISSPELLED

14. A. temporary   B. insistent   C. benificial   14.____
    D. separate   E. NONE MISSPELLED

15. A. achieve   B. dissapoint   C. unanimous   15.____
    D. judgment   E. NONE MISSPELLED

16. A. proceed   B. publicly   C. sincerity   16.____
    D. successful   E. NONE MISSPELLED

17.	A. deceive	B. goverment	C. preferable	17._____
	D. repetitive	E. *NONE MISSPELLED*		
18.	A. emphasis	B. skillful	C. advisible	18._____
	D. optimistic	E. *NONE MISSPELLED*		
19.	A. tendency	B. rescind	C. crucial	19._____
	D. noticable	E. *NONE MISSPELLED*		
20.	A. privelege	B. abbreviate	C. simplify	20._____
	D. divisible	E. *NONE MISSPELLED*		

KEY (CORRECT ANSWERS)

1. B. fundamental
2. D. disappear
3. A. accidentally
4. B. career
5. E. None Misspelled
6. C. advantageous
7. C. guarantee
8. D. announcement
9. B. seize
10. A. postpone
11. B. correspondence
12. D. eligible
13. A. accommodate
14. C. beneficial
15. B. disappoint
16. E. None Misspelled
17. B. government
18. C. advisable
19. D. noticeable
20. A. privilege

TEST 2

DIRECTIONS: In each of the following tests in this part, select the letter of the one MIS-SPELLED word in each of the following groups of words. If no word is misspelled, select the last item, letter E (none misspelled). *PRINT THE LETTER OF THE CORRECT ANSWER IN THE SPACE AT THE RIGHT.*

1. A. typical B. descend C. summarize 1.____
   D. continuel E. *NONE MISSPELLED*

2. A. courageous B. recomend C. omission 2.____
   D. eliminate E. *NONE MISSPELLED*

3. A. compliment B. illuminate C. auxilary 3.____
   D. installation E. *NONE MISSPELLED*

4. A. preliminary B. aquainted C. syllable 4.____
   D. analysis E. *NONE MISSPELLED*

5. A. accustomed B. negligible C. interupted 5.____
   D. bulletin E. *NONE MISSPELLED*

6. A. summoned B. managment C. mechanism 6.____
   D. sequence E. *NONE MISSPELLED*

7. A. commitee B. surprise C. noticeable 7.____
   D. emphasize E. *NONE MISSPELLED*

8. A. occurrance B. likely C. accumulate 8.____
   D. grievance E. grievance

9. A. obstacle B. particuliar C. baggage 9.____
   D. fascinating E. *NONE MISSPELLED*

10. A. innumerable B. seize C. applicant 10.____
    D. dicionery E. *NONE MISSPELLED*

11. A. primary B. mechanic C. referred 11.____
    D. admissible E. *NONE MISSPELLED*

12. A. cessation B. beleif C. aggressive 12.____
    D. allowance E. *NONE MISSPELLED*

13. A. leisure B. authentic C. familiar 13.____
    D. contemptable E. *NONE MISSPELLED*

14. A. volume B. forty C. dilemma 14.____
    D. seldum E. *NONE MISSPELLED*

15. A. discrepancy B. aquisition C. exorbitant 15.____
    D. lenient E. *NONE MISSPELLED*

16. A. simultanous B. penetrate C. revision 16.____
    D. conspicuous E. *NONE MISSPELLED*

17. A. ilegible B. gracious C. profitable 17.____
    D. obedience E. *NONE MISSPELLED*

18. A. manufacturer   B. authorize   C. compelling   18.____
    D. pecular   E. *NONE MISSPELLED*

19. A. anxious   B. rehearsal   C. handicaped   19.____
    D. tendency   E. *NONE MISSPELLED*

20. A. meticulous   B. accompaning C. initiative   20.____
    D. shelves   E. *NONE MISSPELLED*

KEY (CORRECT ANSWERS)

1. D. continual
2. B. recommend
3. C. auxiliary
4. B. acquainted
5. C. interrupted
6. B. management
7. A. committee
8. A. occurrence
9. B. particular
10. D. dictionary
11. E. None Misspelled
12. B. belief
13. D. contemptible
14. D. seldom
15. B. acquisition
16. A. simultaneous
17. A. illegible
18. D. peculiar
19. C. handicapped
20. B. accompanying

TEST 3

DIRECTIONS: In each of the following tests in this part, select the letter of the one MIS-SPELLED word in each of the following groups of words. If no word is misspelled, select the last item, letter E (none misspelled). *PRINT THE LETTER OF THE CORRECT ANSWER IN THE SPACE AT THE RIGHT.*

1. A. grievous   B. dilettante   C. gibberish   1.____
   D. upbraid   E. *NONE MISSPELLED*

2. A. embarrassing   B. playright   C. unmanageable   2.____
   D. symmetrical   E. *NONE MISSPELLED*

3. A. sestet   B. denouement   C. liaison   3.____
   D. tattooing   E. *NONE MISSPELLED*

4. A. prophesied   B. soliliquy   C. supersede   4.____
   D. hemorrhage   E. *NONE MISSPELLED*

5. A. colossal   B. renascent   C. parallel   5.____
   D. omnivorous   E. *NONE MISSPELLED*

6. A. passable   B. dispensable   C. deductable   6.____
   D. irreducible   E. *NONE MISSPELLED*

7. A. guerrila   B. carousal   C. maneuver   7.____
   D. staid   E. *NONE MISSPELLED*

8. A. maintenance   B. mountainous   C. sustenance   8.____
   D. gluttinous   E. *NONE MISSPELLED*

9. A. holocaust   B. irascible   C. buccanneer   9.____
   D. mischievous   E. *NONE MISSPELLED*

10. A. diphthong   B. rhododendron   C. inviegle   10.____
    D. shellacked   E. *NONE MISSPELLED*

11. A. Phillipines   B. currant   C. dietitian   11.____
    D. coercion   E. *NONE MISSPELLED*

12. A. courtesey   B. buoyancy   C. fiery   12.____
    D. shepherd   E. *NONE MISSPELLED*

13. A. censor   B. queue   C. obbligato   13.____
    D. antartic   E. *NONE MISSPELLED*

14. A. chrystal   B. chrysanthemum   C. chrysalis   14.____
    D. chrome   E. *NONE MISSPELLED*

15. A. shreik   B. siege   C. sheik   15.____
    D. sieve   E. *NONE MISSPELLED*

16. A. leisure   B. gladioluses   C. kindergarden   16.____
    D. tonnage   E. *NONE MISSPELLED*

17. A. emminent   B. imminent   C. blatant   17.____
    D. privilege   E. *NONE MISSPELLED*

18. A. diphtheria   B. collander   C. seize   18.____
    D. sleight   E. *NONE MISSPELLED*

19. A. frolicking   B. caramel   C. germaine   19.____
    D. kohlrabi   E. *NONE MISSPELLED*

20. A. dispensable   B. compatable   C. recommend   20.____
    D. feasible   E. *NONE MISSPELLED*

KEY (CORRECT ANSWERS)

1. E. None Misspelled
2. B. playwright
3. E. None Misspelled
4. B. soliloquy
5. E. None Misspelled
6. C. deductible
7. A. guerrilla
8. D. gluttonous
9. C. buccaneer
10. C. inveigle
11. A. Philippines
12. A. courtesy
13. D. antarctic
14. A. crystal
15. A. shriek
16. C. kindergarten
17. A. eminent
18. B. colander
19. C. germane
20. B. compatible

TEST 4

DIRECTIONS: In each of the following tests in this part, select the letter of the one MIS-SPELLED word in each of the following groups of words. If no word is misspelled, select the last item, letter E (none misspelled). *PRINT THE LETTER OF THE CORRECT ANSWER IN THE SPACE AT THE RIGHT.*

1. A. coercion B. rescission C. license 1._____
   D. prophecied E. *NONE MISSPELLED*

2. A. calcimine B. seive C. procedure 2._____
   D. poinsettia E. *NONE MISSPELLED*

3. A. entymology B. echoing C. subtly 3._____
   D. stupefy E. *NONE MISSPELLED*

4. A. mocassin B. assassin C. battalion 4._____
   D. despicable E. *NONE MISSPELLED*

5. A. moustache B. sovereignty C. drunkeness 5._____
   D. staccato E. *NONE MISSPELLED*

6. A. notoriety B. stereotype C. trellis 6._____
   D. Uraguay E. *NONE MISSPELLED*

7. A. hummock B. idiosyncrasy C. licentiate 7._____
   D. plagiarism E. *NONE MISSPELLED*

8. A. denim B. hyssop C. innoculate 8._____
   D. malevolent E. *NONE MISSPELLED*

9. A. boundaries B. corpulency C. gauge 9._____
   D. jingoes E. *NONE MISSPELLED*

10. A. assassin B. refulgeant C. sorghum 10._____
    D. suture E. *NONE MISSPELLED*

11. A. dormatory B. glimpse C. mediocre 11._____
    D. repetition E. *NONE MISSPELLED*

12. A. ambergris B. docility C. loquacious 12._____
    D. Pharoah E. *NONE MISSPELLED*

13. A. curriculum B. ninety-eighth C. occurrence 13._____
    D. repertoire E. *NONE MISSPELLED*

14. A. belladonna B. equable C. immersion 14._____
    D. naphtha E. *NONE MISSPELLED*

15. A. itinerary B. ptomaine C. similar 15._____
    D. solicetous E. *NONE MISSPELLED*

16. A. liquify B. mausoleum C. Philippines 16._____
    D. singeing E. *NONE MISSPELLED*

17. A. descendant B. harrassed C. implausible 17._____
    D. irreverence E. *NONE MISSPELLED*

18.	A. crystallize	B. imperceptible	C. isinglass	18.___
	D. precede	E. *NONE MISSPELLED*		
19.	A. accommodate	B. deferential	C. gazeteer	19.___
	D. plenteous	E. *NONE MISSPELLED*		
20.	A. aching	B. buttress	C. indigenous	20.___
	D. mischievous	E. *NONE MISSPELLED*		

KEY (CORRECT ANSWERS)

1. D. prophesied
2. B. sieve
3. A. entomology
4. A. moccasin
5. C. drunkenness
6. D. Uruguay
7. E. None Misspelled
8. C. inoculate
9. E. None Misspelled
10. B. refulgent
11. A. dormitory
12. D. Pharaoh
13. E. None Misspelled
14. E. None misspelled
15. D. solicitous
16. A. liquefy
17. B. harassed
18. E. None Misspelled
19. C. gazetteer
20. E. None Misspelled

TEST 5

DIRECTIONS: In each of the following tests in this part, select the letter of the one MISSPELLED word in each of the following groups of words. If no word is misspelled, select the last item, letter E (none misspelled). *PRINT THE LETTER OF THE CORRECT ANSWER IN THE SPACE AT THE RIGHT.*

1. A. comensurable B. fracas C. obeisance 1._____
   D. remittent E. *NONE MISSPELLED*

2. A. defiance B. delapidated C. motley 2._____
   D. rueful E. *NONE MISSPELLED*

3. A. demeanor B. epoch C. furtive 3._____
   D. parley E. *NONE MISSPELLED*

4. A. disciples B. influencial C. nemesis 4._____
   D. poultry E. *NONE MISSPELLED*

5. A. decision B. encourage C. incidental 5._____
   D. satyr E. *NONE MISSPELLED*

6. A. collate B. connivance C. luxurient 6._____
   D. manageable E. *NONE MISSPELLED*

7. A. constituencies B. crocheted C. foreclosure 7._____
   D. scintillating E. *NONE MISSPELLED*

8. A. arraignment B. assassination C. carburator 8._____
   D. irrationally E. *NONE MISSPELLED*

9. A. livelihood B. noticeable C. optomiatic 9._____
   D. psychology E. *NONE MISSPELLED*

10. A. daub B. massacre C. repitition 10._____
    D. requiem E. *NONE MISSPELLED*

11. A. adversary B. beneficiary C. cemetery 11._____
    D. desultory E. *NONE MISSPELLED*

12. A. criterion B. elicit C. incredulity 12._____
    D. omnishient E. *NONE MISSPELLED*

13. A. dining B. fiery C. incidentally 13._____
    D. rheumatism E. *NONE MISSPELLED*

14. A. collaborator B. gaudey C. habilitation 14._____
    D. logician E. *NONE MISSPELLED*

15. A. dirge B. ogle C. recumbent 15._____
    D. reminiscence E. *NONE MISSPELLED*

16. A. conscientious B. renunciation C. inconvenient 16._____
    D. inoculate E. *NONE MISSPELLED*

17. A. crystalline B. scimitar C. ecstacy 17._____
    D. vestigial E. *NONE MISSPELLED*

85

18.	A. phlegmatic D. refectory		B. rhythm E. *NONE MISSPELLED*		C. plebescite	18.____
19.	A. resilient D. sobriety		B. resevoir E. *NONE MISSPELLED*		C. recipient	19.____
20.	A. privilege D. basilisk		B. leige E. *NONE MISSPELLED*		C. leisure	20.____

KEY (CORRECT ANSWERS)

1. A. commensurable
2. B. dilapidated
3. E. None Misspelled
4. B. influential
5. E. None Misspelled
6. C. luxuriant
7. E. None Misspelled
8. C. carburetor
9. C. optimistic
10. C. repetition
11. E. None Misspelled
12. D. omniscient
13. E. None Misspelled
14. B. gaudy
15. E. None Misspelled
16. E. None Misspelled
17. C. ecstasy
18. C. plebiscite
19. B. reservoir
20. B. liege

TEST 6

DIRECTIONS: In each of the following tests in this part, select the letter of the one MISSPELLED word in each of the following groups of words. If no word is misspelled, select the last item, letter E (none misspelled). *PRINT THE LETTER OF THE CORRECT ANSWER IN THE SPACE AT THE RIGHT.*

1. A. repellent B. elliptical C. paralelling 1.____
   D. colossal E. *NONE MISSPELLED*

2. A. uproarious B. grievous C. armature 2.____
   D. tabular E. *NONE MISSPELLED*

3. A. ammassed B. embarrassed C. promissory 3.____
   D. asymmetrical E. *NONE MISSPELLED*

4. A. maintenance B. correspondence C. benificence 4.____
   D. miasmic E. *NONE MISSPELLED*

5. A. demurred B. occurrence C. temperament 5.____
   D. abhorrance E. *NONE MISSPELLED*

6. A. proboscis B. lucious C. mischievous 6.____
   D. vilify E. *NONE MISSPELLED*

7. A. feasable B. divisible C. permeable 7.____
   D. forcible E. *NONE MISSPELLED*

8. A. courteous B. venemous C. heterogeneous 8.____
   D. lustrous E. *NONE MISSPELLED*

9. A. millionaire B. mayonnaise C. questionaire 9.____
   D. silhouette E. *NONE MISSPELLED*

10. A. contemptible B. irreverent C. illimitable 10.____
    D. inveigled E. *NONE MISSPELLED*

11. A. prevalent B. irrelavent C. ecstasy 11.____
    D. auxiliary E. *NONE MISSPELLED*

12. A. impeccable B. raillery C. precede 12.____
    D. occurrence E. *NONE MISSPELLED*

13. A. patrolling B. vignette C. ninety 13.____
    D. surveilance E. *NONE MISSPELLED*

14. A. holocaust B. incidently C. weird 14.____
    D. canceled E. *NONE MISSPELLED*

15. A. emmendation B. gratuitous C. fissionable 15.____
    D. dilemma E. *NONE MISSPELLED*

16. A. harass B. innuendo C. capilary 16.____
    D. pachyderm E. *NONE MISSPELLED*

17. A. concomitant B. Lilliputian C. sarcophagus 17.____
    D. melifluous E. *NONE MISSPELLED*

18. A. interpolate B. disident C. venal 18.___
    D. inveigh E. *NONE MISSPELLED*

19. A. supercillious B. biennial C. gargantuan 19.___
    D. irresistible E. *NONE MISSPELLED*

20. A. conniving B. expedite C. inflammible 20.___
    D. incorruptible E. *NONE MISSPELLED*

KEY (CORRECT ANSWERS)

1. C. paralleling
2. E. None Misspelled
3. A. amassed
4. C. beneficence
5. D. abhorrence
6. B. luscious
7. A. feasible
8. B. venomous
9. C. questionnaire
10. E. None Misspelled
11. B. irrelevant
12. E. None Misspelled
13. D. surveillance
14. B. incidentally
15. A. emendation
16. C. capillary
17. D. mellifluous
18. B. dissident
19. A. supercilious
20. C. inflammable

TEST 7

DIRECTIONS: In each of the following tests in this part, select the letter of the one MISSPELLED word in each of the following groups of words. If no word is misspelled, select the last item, letter E (none misspelled). *PRINT THE LETTER OF THE CORRECT ANSWER IN THE SPACE AT THE RIGHT.*

1.	A. torturous D. flaccid	B. omniscient E. NONE MISSPELLED	C. hymenial	1.____
2.	A. seige D. grieve	B. seize E. NONE MISSPELLED	C. frieze	2.____
3.	A. indispensible D. receptacle	B. euphony E. NONE MISSPELLED	C. victuals	3.____
4.	A. schism D. epicurian	B. fortissimo E. NONE MISSPELLED	C. innocuous	4.____
5.	A. sustenance D. rarefy	B. vilefy E. NONE MISSPELLED	C. maintenance	5.____
6.	A. desiccated D. preponderance	B. alleviate E. NONE MISSPELLED	C. beneficence	6.____
7.	A. battalion D. innert	B. incubus E. NONE MISSPELLED	C. sacrilegious	7.____
8.	A. shiboleth D. dichotomy	B. connoisseur E. NONE MISSPELLED	C. potpourri	8.____
9.	A. pamphlet D. benefited	B. similar E. NONE MISSPELLED	C. parlament	9.____
10.	A. genealogy D. abhorrence	B. tyrannical E. NONE MISSPELLED	C. diletante	10.____
11.	A. effeminate D. fission	B. concensus E. NONE MISSPELLED	C. agglomeration	11.____
12.	A. narcissus D. peccadillo	B. lyceum E. NONE MISSPELLED	C. odissey	12.____
13.	A. stupefied D. frieze	B. psychiatry E. NONE MISSPELLED	C. onerous	13.____
14.	A. intelligible D. albumen	B. semaphore E. NONE MISSPELLED	C. pronounciation	14.____
15.	A. annihilate D. allergy	B. tyrannical E. NONE MISSPELLED	C. occurence	15.____
16.	A. gauging D. its	B. probossis E. NONE MISSPELLED	C. specimen	16.____
17.	A. diphthong D. dilemma	B. connoisseur E. NONE MISSPELLED	C. iresistible	17.____

18. A. affect   B. baccillus   C. beige   18._____
    D. seize   E. *NONE MISSPELLED*

19. A. apostasy   B. sustenance   C. synonym   19._____
    D. epigrammatic E. *NONE MISSPELLED*

20. A. discernable B. consul   C. efflorescence   20._____
    D. complement E. *NONE MISSPELLED*

KEY (CORRECT ANSWERS)

1. C. hymeneal
2. A. siege
3. A. indispensable
4. D. epicurean
5. B. vilify
6. E. None Misspelled
7. D. inert
8. A. shibboleth
9. C. parliament
10. C. dilettante
11. B. consensus
12. C. odyssey
13. E. None Misspelled
14. C. pronunciation
15. C. occurrence
16. B. proboscis
17. C. irresistible
18. B. bacillus
19. E. None Misspelled
20. A. discernible

TEST 8

DIRECTIONS: In each of the following tests in this part, select the letter of the one MIS-SPELLED word in each of the following groups of words. If no word is misspelled, select the last item, letter E (none misspelled). *PRINT THE LETTER OF THE CORRECT ANSWER IN THE SPACE AT THE RIGHT.*

1. A. righteous B. seafareing C. colloquial 1.____
   D. contumely E. *NONE MISSPELLED*

2. A. sanitarium B. vicissitude C. mischievious 2.____
   D. chlorophyll E. *NONE MISSPELLED*

3. A. captain B. theirs C. asceticism 3.____
   D. acquiesced E. *NONE MISSPELLED*

4. A. across B. her's C. democracy 4.____
   D. signature E. *NONE MISSPELLED*

5. A. villain B. vacillate C. imposter 5.____
   D. temperament E. *NONE MISSPELLED*

6. A. idyllic B. volitile C. obloquy 6.____
   D. emendation E. *NONE MISSPELLED*

7. A. heinous B. sattelite C. dissident 7.____
   D. ephemeral E. *NONE MISSPELLED*

8. A. ennoble B. shellacked C. vilify 8.____
   D. indissoluble E. *NONE MISSPELLED*

9. A. argueing B. intrepid C. papyrus 9.____
   D. foulard E. *NONE MISSPELLED*

10. A. guttural B. acknowleging C. isosceles 10.____
    D. assonance E. *NONE MISSPELLED*

11. A. shoeing B. exorcise C. development 11.____
    D. irreperable E. *NONE MISSPELLED*

12. A. counseling B. cancellation C. kidnapped 12.____
    D. repellant E. *NONE MISSPELLED*

13. A. disatisfy B. misstep C. usually 13.____
    D. gregarious E. *NONE MISSPELLED*

14. A. unparalleled B. beggar C. embarrass 14.____
    D. ecstacy E. *NONE MISSPELLED*

15. A. descendant B. poliomyelitis C. privilege 15.____
    D. tragedy E. *NONE MISSPELLED*

16. A. nullify B. siderial C. salability 16.____
    D. irrelevant E. *NONE MISSPELLED*

17. A. paraphenalia B. apothecaries C. occurrence 17.____
    D. plagiarize E. *NONE MISSPELLED*

2 (#8)

18. A. asinine B. dissonent C. opossum 18.____
    D. indispensable E. *NONE MISSPELLED*

19. A. orifice B. deferrment C. harass 19.____
    D. accommodate E. *NONE MISSPELLED*

20. A. changeable B. therefor C. incidently 20.____
    D. dissatisfy E. *NONE MISSPELLED*

KEY (CORRECT ANSWERS)

1. B. seafaring
2. C. mischievous
3. E. None Misspelled
4. B. hers
5. C. impostor
6. B. volatile
7. B. satellite
8. E. None Misspelled
9. A. arguing
10. B. acknowledging
11. D. irreparable
12. D. repellent
13. A. dissatisfy
14. D. ecstasy
15. E. None Misspelled
16. B. sidereal
17. A. paraphernalia
18. B. dissonant
19. B. deferment
20. C. incidentally

TEST 9

DIRECTIONS: In each of the following tests in this part, select the letter of the one MIS-SPELLED word in each of the following groups of words. If no word is misspelled, select the last item, letter E (none misspelled). *PRINT THE LETTER OF THE CORRECT ANSWER IN THE SPACE AT THE RIGHT.*

1. A. irreparably B. lovable C. comparitively 1.____
   D. audible E. *NONE MISSPELLED*

2. A. vilify B. efflorescence C. sarcophagus 2.____
   D. sacreligious E. *NONE MISSPELLED*

3. A. picnicking B. proceedure C. hypocrisy 3.____
   D. seize E. *NONE MISSPELLED*

4. A. discomfit B. sapient C. exascerbate 4.____
   D. sarsaparilla E. *NONE MISSPELLED*

5. A. valleys B. maintainance C. abridgment 5.____
   D. reticence E. *NONE MISSPELLED*

6. A. idylic B. beneficent C. singeing 6.____
   D. asterisk E. *NONE MISSPELLED*

7. A. appropos B. violoncello C. peony 7.____
   D. mucilage E. *NONE MISSPELLED*

8. A. caterpillar B. silhouette C. rhapsody 8.____
   D. frieze E. *NONE MISSPELLED*

9. A. appendicitis B. vestigeal C. colonnade 9.____
   D. tortuous E. *NONE MISSPELLED*

10. A. omlet B. diphtheria C. highfalutin 10.____
    D. miniature E. *NONE MISSPELLED*

11. A. diorama B. sustanance C. disastrous 11.____
    D. conscious E. *NONE MISSPELLED*

12. A. inelegible B. irreplaceable C. dissatisfied 12.____
    D. procedural E. *NONE MISSPELLED*

13. A. contemptible B. sacrilegious C. proffessor 13.____
    D. privilege E. *NONE MISSPELLED*

14. A. inoculate B. diptheria C. gladioli 14.____
    D. hypocrisy E. *NONE MISSPELLED*

15. A. pessimism B. ecstasy C. furlough 15.____
    D. vulnerible E. *NONE MISSPELLED*

16. A. supersede B. moccasin C. recondite 16.____
    D. rhythmical E. *NONE MISSPELLED*

17. A. Adirondack B. Phillipines C. Czechoslovakia 17.____
    D. Cincinnati E. *NONE MISSPELLED*

18.	A. weird D. spontaneously		B. impromptu E. *NONE MISSPELLED*		C. guerrila	18.____
19.	A. newstand D. reservoir		B. accidentally E. *NONE MISSPELLED*		C. tangible	19.____
20.	A. macaroni D. giutar		B. mackerel E. *NONE MISSPELLED*		C. ukulele	20.____

KEY (CORRECT ANSWERS)

1. C. comparatively
2. D. sacrilegious
3. B. procedure
4. C. exacerbate
5. B. maintenance
6. A. idyllic
7. A. apropos
8. E. None Misspelled
9. B. vestigial
10. A. omelet
11. B. sustenance
12. A. ineligible
13. C. professor
14. B. diphtheria
15. D. vulnerable
16. E. None Misspelled
17. B. Philippines
18. C. guerrilla
19. A. newsstand
20. D. guitar

TEST 10

DIRECTIONS: In each of the following tests in this part, select the letter of the one MISSPELLED word in each of the following groups of words. If no word is misspelled, select the last item, letter E (none misspelled). *PRINT THE LETTER OF THE CORRECT ANSWER IN THE SPACE AT THE RIGHT.*

1. A. rescission B. sacrament C. hypocricy 1.____
   D. salable E. *NONE MISSPELLED*

2. A. rhythm B. foreboding C. withal 2.____
   D. consciousness E. *NONE MISSPELLED*

3. A. noticeable B. drunkenness C. frolicked 3.____
   D. abcess E. *NONE MISSPELLED*

4. A. supersede B. canoeing C. exorbitant 4.____
   D. vigilance E. *NONE MISSPELLED*

5. A. idiosyncrasy B. pantomine C. isosceles 5.____
   D. wintry E. *NONE MISSPELLED*

6. A. numbskull B. indispensable C. fatiguing 6.____
   D. gluey E. *NONE MISSPELLED*

7. A. dryly B. egregious C. recommend 7.____
   D. irresistable' E. *NONE MISSPELLED*

8. A. unforgettable B. mackeral C. perseverance 8.____
   D. rococo E. *NONE MISSPELLED*

9. A. mischievous B. tyranical C. desiccate 9.____
   D. battalion E. *NONE MISSPELLED*

10. A. accede B. ninth C. abyssmal 10.____
    D. commonalty E. *NONE MISSPELLED*

11. A. resplendent B. colonnade C. harass 11.____
    D. mimicking E. *NONE MISSPELLED*

12. A. dilletante B. pusillanimous C. grievance 12.____
    D. cataclysm E. *NONE MISSPELLED*

13. A. anomaly B. connoisseur C. feasable 13.____
    D. stationery E. *NONE MISSPELLED*

14. A. ennervated B. rescission C. vacillate 14.____
    D. raucous E. *NONE MISSPELLED*

15. A. liquefy B. poniard C. truculant 15.____
    D. weird E. *NONE MISSPELLED*

16. A. existance B. lieutenant C. asinine 16.____
    D. parallelogram E. *NONE MISSPELLED*

17. A. protuberant B. nuisance C. instrumental 17.____
    D. resevoir E. *NONE MISSPELLED*

95

2 (#10)

18. A. sustenance B. pedigree C. supercillious 18.____
    D. clairvoyant E. *NONE MISSPELLED*

19. A. commingle B. bizarre C. gauge 19.____
    D. priviledge E. *NONE MISSPELLED*

20. A. analagous B. irresistible C. apparel 20.____
    D. hindrance E. *NONE MISSPELLED*

KEY (CORRECT ANSWERS)

1. C. hypocrisy
2. E. None Misspelled
3. D. abscess
4. E. None Misspelled
5. B. pantomime
6. A. numskull
7. D. irresistible
8. B. mackerel
9. B. tyrannical
10. C. abysmal
11. E. None Misspelled
12. A. dilettante
13. C. feasible
14. A. enervated
15. C. truculent
16. A. existence
17. D. reservoir
18. C. supercilious
19. D. privilege
20. A. analogous

TEST 11

DIRECTIONS: In each of the following tests in this part, select the letter of the one MISSPELLED word in each of the following groups of words. If no word is misspelled, select the last item, letter E (none misspelled). *PRINT THE LETTER OF THE CORRECT ANSWER IN THE SPACE AT THE RIGHT.*

1. A. impute B. imparshal C. immodest 1.____
   D. imminent E. NONE MISSPELLED

2. A. cover B. audit C. adege 2.____
   D. adder E. NONE MISSPELLED

3. A. promissory B. maturity C. severally 3.____
   D. accomodation E. NONE MISSPELLED

4. A. superintendant B. dependence C. dependents 4.____
   D. entrance E. NONE MISSPELLED

5. A. managable B. navigable C. passable 5.____
   D. laughable E. NONE MISSPELLED

6. A. tolerance B. circumference C. insurance 6.____
   D. dominance E. NONE MISSPELLED

7. A. diameter B. tangent C. paralell 7.____
   D. perimeter E. NONE MISSPELLED

8. A. providential B. personal C. accidental 8.____
   D. diagonel E. NONE MISSPELLED

9. A. ballast B. ballustrade C. allotment 9.____
   D. bourgeois E. NONE MISSPELLED

10. A. diverse B. pedantic C. mishapen 10.____
    D. transient E. NONE MISSPELLED

11. A. surgeon B. sturgeon C. luncheon 11.____
    D. stancheon E. NONE MISSPELLED

12. A. pariah B. estrang C. conceive 12.____
    D. puncilious E. NONE MISSPELLED

13. A. camouflage B. serviceable C. mischievious 13.____
    D. menace E. NONE MISSPELLED

14. A. forefeit B. halve C. hundredth 14.____
    D. illusion E. NONE MISSPELLED

15. A. filial B. arras C. pantomine 15.____
    D. filament E. NONE MISSPELLED

16. A. llama B. madrigal C. martinet 16.____
    D. laxitive E. NONE MISSPELLED

17. A. symtom B. serum C. antiseptic 17.____
    D. aromatic E. NONE MISSPELLED

18.	A. erasable D. laudable	B. irascible E. *NONE MISSPELLED*	C. audable	18._____
19.	A. heroes D. cargos	B. folios E. *NONE MISSPELLED*	C. sopranos	19._____
20.	A. latent D. whose	B. goddess E. *NONE MISSPELLED*	C. aisle	20._____

KEY (CORRECT ANSWERS)

1. B. impartial
2. C. adage
3. D. accommodation
4. A. superintendent
5. A. manageable
6. E. None Misspelled
7. C. parallel
8. D. diagonal
9. B. balustrade
10. C. misshapen
11. D. stanchion
12. B. estrange
13. C. mischievous
14. A. forfeit
15. C. pantomime
16. D. laxative
17. A. symptom
18. C. audible
19. D. cargoes
20. E. None Misspelled

TEST 12

DIRECTIONS: In each of the following tests in this part, select the letter of the one MISSPELLED word in each of the following groups of words. If no word is misspelled, select the last item, letter E (none misspelled). *PRINT THE LETTER OF THE CORRECT ANSWER IN THE SPACE AT THE RIGHT.*

1. A. coconut B. bustling C. abducter 1.____
   D. naphtha E. NONE MISSPELLED

2. A. seriatim B. quadruped C. diphthong 2.____
   D. concensus E. NONE MISSPELLED

3. A. sanction B. propencity C. parabola 3.____
   D. despotic E. NONE MISSPELLED

4. A. circumstantial B. imbroglio C. coalesce 4.____
   D. ductill E. NONE MISSPELLED

5. A. spontaneous B. superlitive C. telepathy 5.____
   D. thesis E. NONE MISSPELLED

6. A. adobe B. apellate C. billion 6.____
   D. chiropody E. NONE MISSPELLED

7. A. combatant B. helium C. esprit de corps 7.____
   D. debillity E. NONE MISSPELLED

8. A. iota B. gopher C. demoralize 8.____
   D. culvert E. NONE MISSPELLED

9. A. invideous B. gourmand C. embryo 9.____
   D. despicable E. NONE MISSPELLED

10. A. dispeptic B. dromedary C. dormant 10.____
    D. duress E. NONE MISSPELLED

11. A. spiggot B. suffrage C. technology 11.____
    D. thermostat E. NONE MISSPELLED

12. A. aberration B. antropology C. bayou 12.____
    D. cashew E. NONE MISSPELLED

13. A. ricochet B. poncho C. oposum 13.____
    D. melee E. NONE MISSPELLED

14. A. semester B. quadrent C. penchant 14.____
    D. mustang E. NONE MISSPELLED

15. A. rhetoric B. polygimy C. optimum 15.____
    D. mendicant E. NONE MISSPELLED

16. A. labyrint B. hegira C. ergot 16.____
    D. debenture E. NONE MISSPELLED

17. A. solvant B. radioactive C. photostat 17.____
    D. nominative E. NONE MISSPELLED

18. A. sporadic   B. excelsior   C. tenible   18.___
    D. thorax   E. *NONE MISSPELLED*

19. A. mischievous   B. bouillon   C. asinine   19.___
    D. alien   E. *NONE MISSPELLED*

20. A. sanguinery   B. prolix   C. harangue   20.___
    D. minutia   E. *NONE MISSPELLED*

KEY (CORRECT ANSWERS)

1. C. abductor
2. D. consensus
3. B. propensity
4. D. ductile
5. B. superlative
6. B. appellate
7. D. debility
8. E. None Misspelled
9. A. invidious
10. A. dyspeptic
11. A. spigot
12. B. anthropology
13. C. opossum
14. B. quadrant
15. B. polygamy
16. A. labyrinth
17. A. solvent
18. C. tenable
19. E. None Misspelled
20. A. sanguinary

TEST 13

DIRECTIONS: In each of the following tests in this part, select the letter of the one MISSPELLED word in each of the following groups of words. If no word is misspelled, select the last item, letter E (none misspelled). *PRINT THE LETTER OF THE CORRECT ANSWER IN THE SPACE AT THE RIGHT.*

1. A. controvert B. cache C. auricle 1._____
    D. impromptu E. NONE MISSPELLED

2. A. labial B. heffer C. intrigue 2._____
    D. decagon E. NONE MISSPELLED

3. A. statistics B. syllable C. tenon 3._____
    D. tituler E. NONE MISSPELLED

4. A. lenient B. migraine C. embarras 4._____
    D. nepotism E. NONE MISSPELLED

5. A. lichen B. horoscope C. orthadox 5._____
    D. pageant E. NONE MISSPELLED

6. A. libretto B. humis C. fallacy 6._____
    D. dextrose E. NONE MISSPELLED

7. A. clinical B. alimoney C. bourgeois 7._____
    D. proverbial E. NONE MISSPELLED

8. A. dictator B. clipper C. braggadoccio 8._____
    D. assuage E. NONE MISSPELLED

9. A. reverence B. hydraulic C. felon 9._____
    D. diaphram E. NONE MISSPELLED

10. A. retrobution B. polyp C. optician 10._____
    D. mentor E. NONE MISSPELLED

11. A. resonant B. helicopter C. rejoicing 11._____
    D. decisive E. NONE MISSPELLED

12. A. renigade B. restitution C. faculty 12._____
    D. devise E. NONE MISSPELLED

13. A. solicitors B. gratuitous C. spherical 13._____
    D. crusible E. NONE MISSPELLED

14. A. spongy B. ramify C. pica 14._____
    D. noxtious E. NONE MISSPELLED

15. A. automaton B. cadence C. consummate 15._____
    D. ancillery E. NONE MISSPELLED

16. A. magnanimous B. iminent C. tonsillitis 16._____
    D. dowager E. NONE MISSPELLED

17. A. aerial B. apprehend C. bilinear 17._____
    D. transum E. NONE MISSPELLED

18.	A. vacuum D. warbler	B. idiom E. *NONE MISSPELLED*	C. veriety	18.____
19.	A. zephyr D. nonpareil	B. rarify E. *NONE MISSPELLED*	C. physiology	19.____
20.	A. risque D. meridian	B. posterity E. *NONE MISSPELLED*	C. opus	20.____

KEY (CORRECT ANSWERS)

1. E. None Misspelled
2. B. heifer
3. D. titular
4. C. embarrass
5. C. orthodox
6. B. humus
7. B. alimony
8. C. braggadocio
9. D. diaphragm
10. A. retribution
11. E. None Misspelled
12. A. renegade
13. D. crucible
14. D. noxious
15. D. ancillary
16. B. imminent
17. D. transom
18. C. variety
19. B. rarefy
20. D. meridian

TEST 14

DIRECTIONS: In each of the following tests in this part, select the letter of the one MIS-SPELLED word in each of the following groups of words. If no word is misspelled, select the last item, letter E (none misspelled). *PRINT THE LETTER OF THE CORRECT ANSWER IN THE SPACE AT THE RIGHT.*

1. A. pygmy B. seggregation C. clayey 1.____
   D. homogeneous E. *NONE MISSPELLED*

2. A. homeopathy B. predelection C. hindrance 2.____
   D. guillotine E. *NONE MISSPELLED*

3. A. cumulative B. dandelion C. incission 3.____
   D. malpractice E. *NONE MISSPELLED*

4. A. paradise B. allegiance C. frustrate 4.____
   D. impecunious E. *NONE MISSPELLED*

5. A. licquor B. mousse C. exclamatory 5.____
   D. disciple E. *NONE MISSPELLED*

6. A. lame B. winesome C. valvular 6.____
   D. unadvised E. *NONE MISSPELLED*

7. A. Terre Haute B. Cyrano de Bergerac C. Stamboul 7.____
   D. Roosvelt E. *NONE MISSPELLED*

8. A. perambulator B. ruminate C. litturgy 8.____
   D. staple E. *NONE MISSPELLED*

9. A. hectic B. inpregnate C. otter 9.____
   D. muscat E. *NONE MISSPELLED*

10. A. lighterage B. lumbar C. insurence 10.____
    D. monsoon E. *NONE MISSPELLED*

11. A. lethal B. iliterateness C. manifold 11.____
    D. minuet E. *NONE MISSPELLED*

12. A. forfeit B. halve C. hundredth 12.____
    D. illusion E. *NONE MISSPELLED*

13. A. dissolute B. conundrum C. fallacious 13.____
    D. descrimination E. *NONE MISSPELLED*

14. A. diva B. codicile C. expedient 14.____
    D. garrison E. *NONE MISSPELLED*

15. A. filial B. arras C. pantomine 15.____
    D. filament E. *NONE MISSPELLED*

16. A. inveigle B. paraphenalia C. archivist 16.____
    D. complexion E. *NONE MISSPELLED*

17. A. dessicate B. ambidextrous C. meritorious 17.____
    D. revocable E. *NONE MISSPELLED*

103

18. A. queue B. isthmus C. committal 18.___
    D. binnocular E. *NONE MISSPELLED*

19. A. changeable B. abbreviating C. regretable 19.___
    D. japanned E. *NONE MISSPELLED*

20. A. Saskechewan B. Bismarck C. Albuquerque 20.___
    D. Apennines E. *NONE MISSPELLED*

KEY (CORRECT ANSWERS)

1. B. segregation
2. B. predilection
3. C. incision
4. E. None Misspelled
5. A. liquor
6. B. winsome
7. D. Roosevelt
8. C. liturgy
9. B. impregnate
10. C. insurance
11. B. illiterateness
12. E. None Misspelled
13. D. discrimination
14. B. codicil
15. C. pantomime
16. B. paraphernalia
17. A. desiccate
18. D. binocular
19. C. regrettable
20. A. Saskatchewan

TEST 15

DIRECTIONS: In each of the following tests in this part, select the letter of the one MIS-SPELLED word in each of the following groups of words. If no word is misspelled, select the last item, letter E (none misspelled). *PRINT THE LETTER OF THE CORRECT ANSWER IN THE SPACE AT THE RIGHT.*

1. A. culinery   B. millinery   C. humpbacked   1.____
   D. improvise E. *NONE MISSPELLED*

2. A. Brittany   B. embarrassment   C. coifure   2.____
   D. leveled   E. *NONE MISSPELLED*

3. A. minnion   B. aborgine   C. antagonism   3.____
   D. arabesque E. *NONE MISSPELLED*

4. A. tractible B. camouflage   C. permanent   4.____
   D. dextrous   E. *NONE MISSPELLED*

5. A. inequitous B. kilowatt   C. weasel   5.____
   D. lunging   E. *NONE MISSPELLED*

6. A. palatable B. odious   C. motif   6.____
   D. Maltese   E. *NONE MISSPELLED*

7. A. Beau Brummel   B. Febuary   C. Bedouin   7.____
   D. Damascus   E. *NONE MISSPELLED*

8. A. llama   B. madrigal   C. illitive   8.____
   D. marlin   E. *NONE MISSPELLED*

9. A. babboon   B. dossier   C. esplanade   9.____
   D. frontispiece   E. *NONE MISSPELLED*

10. A. thrashing B. threshing   C. atavism   10.____
    D. artifect E. *NONE MISSPELLED*

11. A. ballast   B. ballustrade   C. allotment   11.____
    D. bourgeois E. *NONE MISSPELLED*

12. A. amenuensis B. saccharine   C. hippopotamus   12.____
    D. rhinoceros E. *NONE MISSPELLED*

13. A. maintenance B. bullion   C. khaki   13.____
    D. libarian E. *NONE MISSPELLED*

14. A. diverse   B. pedantic   C. mishapen   14.____
    D. transient E. *NONE MISSPELLED*

15. A. exhilirate B. avaunt   C. avocado   15.____
    D. avocation E. *NONE MISSPELLED*

16. A. narcotic B. flippancy   C. daffodil   16.____
    D. narcisus E. *NONE MISSPELLED*

17. A. inflamation B. disfranchisement   C. surmise   17.____
    D. adviser   E. *NONE MISSPELLED*

2 (#15)

18. A. syphon   B. inquiry   C. shanghaied   18.____
    D. collapsible   E. *NONE MISSPELLED*

19. A. occassionally   B. antecedence   C. reprehensible   19.____
    D. inveigh   E. *NONE MISSPELLED*

20. A. crescendos   B. indispensible   C. mosquitoes   20.____
    D. impeccable   E. *NONE MISSPELLED*

KEY (CORRECT ANSWERS)

1. A. culinary
2. C. coiffure
3. A. minion
4. A. tractable
5. A. iniquitous
6. E. None Misspelled
7. B. February
8. D. illative
9. A. baboon
10. D. artifact
11. B. balustrade
12. A. amanuensis
13. D. librarian
14. C. misshapen
15. A. exhilarate
16. D. narcissus
17. A. inflammation
18. E. None Misspelled
19. A. occasionally
20. B. indispensable

NAME AND NUMBER CHECKING
EXAMINATION SECTION
TEST 1

DIRECTIONS: This test is designed to measure your speed/and accuracy. You are urged to work both quickly and accurately and to do correctly as many lists as you can in the time allowed. The test consists of lists or pairs of names and numbers. Count the number of IDENTICAL pairs in each list. Then, select the correct number, 1, 2, 3, 4, 5, and indicate your choice in the space at the right. Two sample questions are presented for your guidance, together with the correct solutions.

SAMPLE LIST A
Adelphi College – Adelphia College
Braxton Corp – Braxeton Corp.
Wassaic State School – Wassaic State School
Central Islip State Hospital – Central Isllip State Hospital
Greenwich House – Greenwich House

NOTE: There are only two correct pairs—Wassaic State School and Greenwich House. Therefore, the CORRECT answer is 2.

SAMPLE LIST B
78453694 – 78453684
784530 – 784530
533 – 534
67845 – 67845
2368745 – 2368755

NOTE: There are only two correct pairs—784530 and 67845. Therefore, the CORRECT answer is 2.

LIST 1   1.____
    Diagnostic Clinic   – Diagnostic Clinic
    Yorkville Health   – Yorkville Health
    Meinhard Clinic   – Meinhart Clinic
    Corlears Clinic   – Carlears Clinic
    Tremont Diagnostic – Tremont Diagnostic

LIST 2   2.____
    73526   – 73526
    7283627198   – 7283627198
    627   – 637
    728352617283   – 7283526178282
    6281   – 6281

2 (#1)

LIST 3   3.____
    Jefferson Clinic   – Jeffersen Clinic
    Mott Haven Center   – Mott Havan Center
    Bronx Hospital   – Bronx Hospital
    Montefiore Hospital   – Montifeore Hospital
    Beth Isreal Hospital   – Beth Israel Hospital

LIST 4   4.____
    936271826   – 936371826
    5271   – 5291
    82637192037   – 82637192037
    527182   – 5271882
    726354256   - 72635456

LIST 5   5.____
    Trinity Hospital   – Trinity Hospital
    Central Harlem   – Centrel Harlem
    St. Luke's Hospital   – St. Lukes' Hospital
    Mt. Sinai Hospital   – Mt. Sinia Hospital
    N.Y. Dispensery   – N.Y. Dispensary

LIST 6   6.____
    725361552637   – 725361555637
    7526378   – 7526377
    6975   – 6975
    82637481028   – 82637481028
    3427   – 3429

LIST 7   7.____
    Misericordia Hospital   – Miseracordia Hospital
    Lebonan Hospital   – Lebanon Hospital
    Gouverneur Hospital   – Gouverner Hospital
    German Polyclinic   – German Policlinic
    French Hospital   – French Hospital

LIST 8   8.____
    8277364933251   – 827364933351
    63728   – 63728
    367281   – 367281
    62733846273   – 6273846293
    62836   - 6283

LIST 9   9.____
    King's County Hospital   – Kings County Hospital
    St. Johns Long Island   – St. John's Long Island
    Bellevue Hospital   – Bellvue Hospital
    Beth David Hospital   – Beth David Hospital
    Samaritan Hospital   – Samariton Hospital

LIST 10
		10.____
62836454	– 62836455	
42738267	– 42738369	
573829	– 573829	
738291627874	– 738291627874	
725	- 735	

LIST 11
		11.____
Bloomingdal Clinic	– Bloomingdale Clinic	
Communitty Hospital	– Community Hospital	
Metroplitan Hospital	– Metropoliton Hospital	
Lenox Hill Hospital	– Lonex Hill Hospital	
Lincoln Hospital	– Lincoln Hospital	

LIST 12
		12.____
6283364728	– 6283648	
627385	– 627383	
54283902	– 54283602	
63354	– 63354	
7283562781	- 7283562781	

LIST 13
		13.____
Sydenham Hospital	– Sydanham Hospital	
Roosevalt Hospital	– Roosevelt Hospital	
Vanderbilt Clinic	– Vanderbild Clinic	
Women's Hospital	– Woman's Hospital	
Flushing Hospital	– Flushing Hospital	

LIST 14
		14.____
62738	– 62738	
727355542321	– 72735542321	
263849332	– 263849332	
262837	– 263837	
47382912	- 47382922	

LIST 15
		15.____
Episcopal Hospital	– Episcapal Hospital	
Flower Hospital	– Flouer Hospital	
Stuyvesent Clinic	– Stuyvesant Clinic	
Jamaica Clinic	– Jamaica Clinic	
Ridgwood Clinic	– Ridgewood Clinic	

LIST 16
		16.____
628367299	– 628367399	
111	– 111	
118293304829	– 1182839489	
4448	– 4448	
333693678	- 333693678	

LIST 17
Arietta Crane Farm	– Areitta Crane Farm	17.____
Bikur Chilim Home	– Bikur Chilom Home	
Burke Foundation	– Burke Foundation	
Blythedale Home	– Blythdale Home	
Campbell Cottages	– Cambell Cottages	

LIST 18
32123	– 32132	18.____
273893326783	– 27389326783	
473829	– 473829	
7382937	– 7383937	
3628890122332	- 36289012332	

LIST 19
Caraline Rest	– Caroline Rest	19.____
Loreto Rest	– Loretto Rest	
Edgewater Creche	– Edgwater Creche	
Holiday Farm	– Holiday Farm	
House of St. Giles	– House of st. Giles	

LIST 20
557286777	– 55728677	20.____
3678902	– 3678892	
1567839	– 1567839	
7865434712	– 7865344712	
9927382	- 9927382	

LIST 21
Isabella Home	– Isabela Home	21.____
James A. Moore Home	– James A. More Home	
The Robin's Nest	– The Roben's Nest	
Pelham Home	– Pelam Home	
St. Eleanora's Home	– St. Eleanora's Home	

LIST 22
273648293048	– 273648293048	22.____
334	– 334	
7362536478	– 7362536478	
7362819273	– 7362819273	
7362	- 7363	

LIST 23
St. Pheobe's Mission	– St. Phebe's Mission	23.____
Seaside Home	– Seaside Home	
Speedwell Society	– Speedwell Society	
Valeria Home	– Valera Home	
Wiltwyck	- Wildwyck	

5 (#1)

LIST 24
    63728   – 63738
    63728192736   – 63728192738
    428   – 458
    62738291527   – 62738291529
    63728192   - 63728192

24.____

LIST 25
    McGaffin   – McGafin
    David Ardslee   – David Ardslee
    Axton Supply   – Axeton Supply Co
    Alice Russell   – Alice Russell
    Dobson Mfg. Co.   – Dobsen Mfg. Co.

25.____

KEY (CORRECT ANSWERS)

1.	3		11.	1
2.	3		12.	2
3.	1		13.	1
4.	1		14.	2
5.	1		15.	1
6.	2		16.	3
7.	1		17.	1
8.	2		18.	1
9.	1		19.	1
10.	2		20.	2

21.	1
22.	4
23.	2
24.	1
25.	2

TEST 2

DIRECTIONS: This test is designed to measure your speed/and accuracy. You are urged to work both quickly and accurately and to do correctly as many lists as you can in the time allowed. The test consists of lists or pairs of names and numbers. Count the number of IDENTICAL pairs in each list. Then, select the correct number, 1, 2, 3, 4, 5, and indicate your choice in the space at the right.

LIST 1   1.____
    82637381028   – 82637281028
    928   – 928
    72937281028   – 72937281028
    7362   – 7362
    927382615   – 927382615

LIST 2   2.____
    Albee Theatre   – Albee Theatre
    Lapland Lumber Co.   – Laplund Lumber Co.
    Adelphi College   – Adelphi College
    Jones & Son Inc.   – Jones & Sons Inc.
    S.W. Ponds Co.   – S.W. Ponds Co.

LIST 3   3.____
    85345   – 85345
    895643278   – 895643277
    726352   – 726353
    632685   – 632685
    7263524   – 7236524

LIST 4   4.____
    Eagle Library   – Eagle Library
    Dodge Ltd.   – Dodge Co.
    Stromberg Carlson   – Stromberg Carlsen
    Clairice Ling   – Clairice Linng
    Mason Book Co.   – Matson Book Co.

LIST 5   5.____
    66273   – 66273
    629   – 629
    7382517283   – 7382517283
    637281   – 639281
    2738261   – 2788261

LIST 6   6.____
    Robert MacColl   – Robert McColl
    Buick Motor   – Buck Motors
    Murray Bay & Co. Ltd.   – Murray Bay Co. Ltd.
    L.T. Ltyle   – L.T. Lyttle
    A.S. Landas   – A.S. Landas

LIST 7
		7.____
6271526374890	– 627152637490	
73526189	– 73526189	
5372	– 5392	
637281142	– 63728124	
4783946	– 4783046	

LIST 8
		8.____
Tyndall Burke	– Tyndell Burke	
W. Briehl	– W. Briehl	
Burritt Publishing Co.	– Buritt Publishing Co.	
Frederick Breyer & Co.	– Frederick Breyer Co.	
Bailey Buulard	– Bailey Bullard	

LIST 9
		9.____
634	– 634	
16837	– 163837	
273892223678	– 27389223678	
527182	– 527782	
3628901223	– 3629002223	

LIST 10
		10.____
Ernest Boas	– Ernest Boas	
Rankin Barne	– Rankin Barnes	
Edward Appley	– Edward Appely	
Camel	– Camel	
Caiger Food Co.	– Caiger Food Co.	

LIST 11
		11.____
6273	– 6273	
322	– 332	
15672839	– 15672839	
63728192637	– 63728192639	
738	– 738	

LIST 12
		12.____
Wells Fargo Co.	– Wells Fargo Co.	
W.D. Brett	– W.D. Britt	
Tassco Co.	– Tassko Co.	
Republic Mills	– Republic Mill	
R.W. Burnham	– R.W. Burhnam	

LIST 13
		13.____
7253529152	– 7283529152	
6283	– 6383	
52839102738	– 5283910238	
308	– 398	
82637201927	– 8263720127	

LIST 14
Schumacker Co.	– Shumacker Co.
C.H. Caiger	– C.H. Caiger
Abraham Strauss	– Abram Straus
B.F. Boettjer	– B.F. Boettijer
Cut-Rate Store	– Cut-Rate Stores

14.____

LIST 15
15273826	– 15273826
72537	– 73537
726391027384	– 62639107384
637389	– 627399
725382910	– 725382910

15.____

LIST 16
Hixby Ltd.	– Hixby Lt'd.
S. Reiner	– S. Riener
Reynard Co.	– Reynord Co.
Esso Gassoline Co.	– Esso Gasolene Co.
Belle Brock	– Belle Brock

16.____

LIST 17
7245	– 7245
819263728192	– 819263728172
682537289	– 682537298
789	– 789
82936542891	– 82936542891

17.____

LIST 18
Joseph Cartwright	– Joseph Cartwrite
Foote Food Co.	– Foot Food Co.
Weiman & Held	– Weiman & Held
Sanderson Shoe Co.	– Sandersen Shoe Co.
A.M. Byrne	– A.N. Byrne

18.____

LIST 19
4738267	– 4738277
63728	– 63729
6283628901	– 6283628991
918264	– 918264
263728192037	– 2637728192073

19.____

LIST 20
Exray Laboratories	– Exray Labratories
Curley Toy Co.	– Curly Toy Co.
J. Lauer & Cross	– J. Laeur & Cross
Mireco Brands	– Mireco Brands
Sandor Lorand	– Sandor Larand

20.____

4 (#2)

LIST 21   21.____
- 607   – 609
- 6405   – 6403
- 976   – 996
- 101267   – 101267
- 2065432   – 20965432

LIST 22   22.____
- John Macy & Sons   – John Macy & Son
- Venus Pencil Co.   – Venus Pencil Co.
- Nell McGinnis   – Nell McGinnis
- McCutcheon & Co.   – McCutcheon & Co.
- Sun-Tan Oil   – Sun-Tan Oil

LIST 23   23.____
- 703345700   – 703345700
- 46754   – 466754
- 3367490   – 3367490
- 3379   – 3778
- 47384   – 47394

LIST 24   24.____
- arthritis   – arthritis
- asthma   – asthma
- endocrine   – endocrene
- gastro-enterological   – gastrol-enteralogical
- orthopedic   – orthopedic

LIST 25   25.____
- 743829432   – 743828432
- 998   – 998
- 732816253902   – 732816252902
- 46829   – 46830
- 7439120249   – 7439210249

KEY (CORRECT ANSWERS)

1.	4	11.	3
2.	3	12.	1
3.	2	13.	1
4.	1	14.	1
5.	2	15.	2
6.	1	16.	1
7.	2	17.	3
8.	1	18.	1
9.	1	19.	1
10.	3	20.	1

21. 1
22. 4
23. 2
24. 3
25. 1

FILING

EXAMINATION SECTION
TEST 1

DIRECTIONS: For each of the following, you are given a name above and three other names in alphabetical order below. The letters A, B, C, and D stand for spaces where you could file the name. Find the CORRECT space for the name given above so that it will be in alphabetical order with the names below it. The letter that stands for that space is the answer to the question.

1. CURRAN, THOMAS
   A CURLEY, MARY B CURR, SAMUEL C CURREN, KATIE D

2. KAPLIN, EDWIN
   A KAPLEN, MICHAEL B KAPLIN, JULIA C KAPLON, DAVID D

3. PENSKY, LEONA
   A PENSLER, SANDY B PENSLEY, JOEL C PENSLEY, JOSEPH D

4. ROWEN, MARCIA
   A ROWEN, CHRISTOPHER B ROWEN, LOUIS C ROWEN, MARTIN D

5. FOSTER, GRACE
   A FOSS, EARL B FOSSE, NICHOLE C FOSTER, KEITH D

6. KO, FAI
   A KO, HOK B KO, HUNG-FAI C KO, HYUN JUNG D

7. MICHALIK, ANTHONY
   A MICHALIC, GARY B MICHALIS, HELEN C MICHALK, KLAUS D

8. MINTZ, JUDITH
   A MINTZ, JAKE B MINTZ, JAMES C MINTZ, JULIUS D

9. POWERS, ANN
   A POUST, THERESE B POWELL, LUTHER C POWER, RACHEL D

10. PRACTICAL STUDIO, INC.
    A PRACTICAL PUBLISHING B PRACTICE DEVELOPMENT C PRACTICE SERVICE CORP. D

11. SHERWIN, ROBERTA
    A SHERWIN, RAUL B SHERWIN, RICHARD C SHERWIN, ROBERT D

12. JACOBSEN, JENNIFER
    A JACOBSON, PETER B JACOBY, JACK C JACOVITZ, GAIL D

13. BLEINHEIM, GLORIA
    A BLELOCK, JULIA B BLENCOWE, FRED C BLENMAN, ANTHONY D

14. FIRST STERLING CORP.   14.____
    A FIRST STATE PRODUCTS B FIRST STEP INC. C FIRST STOP CORP. D

15. VICKERS, GEORGE   15.____
    A VICHEY, LOUIS B VICHI, MARIO C VICKI, SUSAN D

16. STEIN, DAVID   16.____
    A STEIN, CRAIG B STEIN, DANIEL C STEIN, DEBORAH D

17. IGLESIAS, BERNADETTE   17.____
    A IGER, MARTIN B IGLEHEART, PHYLICIA C IGLEWSKI, RICHARD D

18. IDEAL ROOFING CORP.   18.____
    A IDEAL REPRODUCTION B IDEAL RESTAURANT C IDEAL RUBBER PRODUCTS
    D

19. TODARO, JOSEPH   19.____
    A TODD, ANNE B TODE, WALLY C TODMAN, JUDITH D

20. WILKERSON, RUTH   20.____
    A WILKENS, FRANK B WILKES, BARRY C WILKIE, JANE D

21. HUGHES, MARY   21.____
    A HUGHES, MANUEL B HUGHES, MARGARET C HUGHES, MARTHA D

22. GODWIN, JAMES   22.____
    A GODFREY, SONDRA B GODMAN, GABRIEL C GODREAU, ROBERT D

23. NACHMAN, DAVID   23.____
    A NACHT, JAMES B NACK, SAUL C NACKENSON, LORI D

24. CASPER, LAURENCE   24.____
    A CASPER, LEONARD B CASPER, LESTER C CASPER, LINDA D

25. CULEN, ELLEN   25.____
    A CULHANE, JOHN B CULICHI, RADU C CULIN, TERRY D

KEY (CORRECT ANSWERS)

1. C
2. B
3. A
4. C
5. C

6. A
7. B
8. C
9. D
10. B

11. D
12. A
13. A
14. C
15. C

16. C
17. C
18. C
19. A
20. B

21. D
22. D
23. A
24. A
25. A

TEST 2

DIRECTIONS: For each of the following, you are given a name above and three other names in alphabetical order below. The letters A, B, C, and D stand for spaces where you could file the name. Find the CORRECT space for the name given above so that it will be in alphabetical order with the names below it. The letter that stands for that space is the answer to the question.

1. HARMAN, HENRY
   A HARLEY, LILLIAN B HARMER, RALPH C HARMON, CECIL D

2. MANNING, JOHNSON
   A MANNING, JAMES B MANNING, JEROME C MANNING, JOHN D

3. NOGUCHI, JANICE
   A NOEL, WALTER B NOGUET, DANIELLE C NOH, DAVID D

4. PARRON, ALFONSE
   A PARRIS, LEON B PARRISH, LINDA C PARROTT, BETTY D

5. GROSS, ELANA
   A GROSS, ELAINE B GROSS, ELIZABETH C GROSS, ELLIOT D

6. HORSTMANN, ANNA
   A HORSMAN, ALLAN B HORST, VALERIE C HORSTMAN, JAMES D

7. JONES, EMILY
   A JONES, ELMA B JONES, ELOISE C JONES, EMMA D

8. LESSING, FRED
   A LESSER, MARTHA B LESSIN, ELLIE C LESSNER, ERWIN D

9. ROSENBLUM, JULIUS
   A ROSENBLUTH, SYLVIA B ROSENBORG, ERIC C ROSENBURG, JANE D

10. YOUNG, THEODORE
    A YOUNG, TERRY B YOUNG, THELMA C YOUNG, THOMAS D

11. RENICK, KAREN
    A RENIE, JOSEPH B RENITA, JOSE C RENKO, DORIS D

12. ADLER, HELEN
    A ADLER, HAROLD B ADLER, HARRY C ADLER, HENRY D

13. BURKHARDT, ANN
    A BURKET, HARRIET B BURKHOLDER, CARL C BURKHOLZ, SCOTT D

14. DE LUCA, PAUL
    A DE LUCA, JOHN B DE LUCIA, AUDREY C DE LUCIA, ROBERT D

15. DEMBSKI, STEPHEN
    A DEMBLING, JOAN B DEMBNER, PETER C DEMBROW, HELEN D

16. FLYNN, ARCHIE   16._____
    A FLYNN, AGNES B FLYNN, ANDREW C FLYNN, ANNMARIE D

17. GRAFFY, PAUL   17._____
    A GRAFMAN, ANDREW B GRAFSTEIN, BETTY C GRAFTON, MELVIN D

18. KERMIT, FRANK   18._____
    A KERMAN, LINDA B KERMISH, RHODA C KERMOYAN, MICKI D

19. METZLER, MAURICE   19._____
    A METZGER, ALFRED B METZIER, SONIA C METZINGER, PAUL D

20. PADDINGTON, TIMOTHY   20._____
    A PADDEN, MICHAEL B PADDISON, BRUCE C PADELL, EUNICE D

21. RICHARDSON, BLANCHE   21._____
    A RICHARDSON, BETTY B RICHARDSON, BEVERLY C RICHARDSON, BRENDA D

22. ISEKI, EMILE   22._____
    A ISELIN, CAROL B ISEN, RICHARD C ISENEE, CYNTHIA D

23. CONNELL, EUGENE   23._____
    A CONNELL, EDWARD B CONNELL, HELEN C CONNELL, HUGH D

24. MAC LEOD, LAURIE   24._____
    A MAC LEOD, LORNA B MC LANE, PAUL C MC LAREN, DUNCAN D

25. BOLE, KENNETH   25._____
    A BOLDEN, ROSIE B BOLDT, LINDA C BOLELLA, DENNIS D

KEY (CORRECT ANSWERS)

1.	B		11.	A
2.	D		12.	C
3.	B		13.	B
4.	C		14.	B
5.	B		15.	D
6.	D		16.	D
7.	C		17.	A
8.	C		18.	C
9.	A		19.	D
10.	C		20.	B

21.	C
22.	A
23.	B
24.	A
25.	C

TEST 3

DIRECTIONS: For each of the following, you are given a name above and three other names in alphabetical order below. The letters A, B, C, and D stand for spaces where you could file the name. Find the CORRECT space for the name given above so that it will be in alphabetical order with the names below it. The letter that stands for that space is the answer to the question.

1. CARLISLE, ALAN
   A CARLINSKY, LEONA B CARLITOS, JUAN C CARLL, CHARLES D

   1.____

2. COLLINS, KAREN
   A COLLINS, KATHLEEN B COLLINS, KATHRYN C COLLINS, KAY D

   2.____

3. GALLOTTI, OSCAR
   A GALLONTY, FRANCIS B GALLOP, LILLIAN C GALLOU, ALEXIS D

   3.____

4. MAHADY, JOHN
   A MAHADEO, PRATAB B MAHAJAN, ASHA C MAHARAJAH, MIARIAM D

   4.____

5. WINGATE, REBECCA
   A WINGARD, LUCILLE B WINGAT, ROBERT C WINGER, HOLLY D

   5.____

6. ZWEIGHAFT, FREDA
   A ZWEIG, BERTRAM B ZWEIGBAUM, BENJAMIN C ZWEIGENTHAL, DOROTHY D

   6.____

7. MAXWELL, GEORGE
   A MAXWELL, EDWARD B MAXWELL, FRANK C MAXWELL, HARRIS D

   7.____

8. O'DOHERTY, SALLY
   A ODETTE, CHARLES B ODIOTTI, MASSIE C ODNORALOV, MIKHAEL D

   8.____

9. JAMES, ROGER
   A JAMIESON, KELLY B JAMNER, ELIZABETH C JAMPOLSKY, MILTON D

   9.____

10. PADIN, FRANCIS
    A PADILLA, ANGELA B PADINGER, JENNY C PADLEY, RAYMOND D

    10.____

11. AAARMAN, ALEC
    A AABY, JANE B AACH, ALBERT C AACHEN, HENRY D

    11.____

12. BILLHARDT, PHILIP
    A BILLERA, FRANKLIN B BILLIG, LESLIE C BILLINGS, CAROL D

    12.____

13. LADEROS, ELANA
    A LADENHEIM, HELENE B LADERMAN, SAM C LADHA, SANDRA D

    13.____

14. PUCKERING, DENNIS
    A PUCKETT, AUDREY B PUCKNAT, JOHN C PUCKO, BENNY D

    14.____

15. SCHOLZE, GEORGE
    A SCHOLNICK, LEONARD B SCHOLOSS, JACK C SCHOLZ, PAUL D

    15.____

16. WILSON, MERYL 16._____
    A WILSON, MERIMAN B WILSON, MERRY C WILSON, MERRYL D

17. ZUKOWSKI, MICHAEL 17._____
    A ZWACK, ALEXA B ZYKO, KATHERINE C ZYMAN, HERBERT D

18. MC CANNA, THOMAS 18._____
    A MC CANN, GERALD B MC CANNA, JANET C MC CANTS, MOLLIE D

19. PHILIPP, SUSANE 19._____
    A PHILIP, PETER B PHILIPOSE, ANDREW C PHILIPPE, BEATRICE D

20. KINGPIN, PAUL 20._____
    A KINGDON, KENNETH B KINGMAN, JEAN C KINGOLD, RICHARD D

21. HAMILTON, DONALD 21._____
    A HAMILTON, DON B HAMILTON, DOROTHY C HAMILTON, DOUGLAS D

22. BAEL, ELAINE 22._____
    A BAELE, GUSTAVE B BAEN, JAMES C BAENA, ARIEL D

23. BILL, KASEY 23._____
    A BILGINER, NATHAN B BILKAY, WILLIAM C BILLES, BRADFORD D

24. CARLEN, ELLIOT 24._____
    A CARINO, NAN B CARLE, JOHN C CARLESI, ANTHONY D

25. LOURIE, DONALD 25._____
    A LOUIE, ROSE B LOUIS, STEVE C LOVE, MARCIA D

KEY (CORRECT ANSWERS)

1.	B	11.	A
2.	A	12.	B
3.	C	13.	C
4.	B	14.	A
5.	C	15.	D
6.	D	16.	D
7.	C	17.	A
8.	D	18.	C
9.	A	19.	C
10.	B	20.	D

21. B
22. A
23. C
24. C
25. C

TEST 4

DIRECTIONS: For each of the following, you are given a name above and three other names in alphabetical order below. The letters A, B, C, and D stand for spaces where you could file the name. Find the CORRECT space for the name given above so that it will be in alphabetical order with the names below it. The letter that stands for that space is the answer to the question.

1. DEMOPOULOS, GUS
   A DEMOPOULOS, DIMITRI B DEMOPOULOS, HELEN C DEMOPOULOS, LAURA D

2. DRUMWRIGHT, BRUCE
   A DRUMMOND, RANDY B DRUMMUND, WALTER C DRUMRIGHT, JULIUS D

3. GRAHAM, LETICIA
   A GRAHAM, LEON B GRAHAM, LEROY C GRAHAM, LESLIE D

4. KELLEHER, KEVIN
   A KELLARD, WILLIAM B KELLEDY, JAMES C KELLEHER, KRISTINE D

5. LIANG, JAN
   A LIANG, JIE B LIANG, JIN CHANG C LIANG, JIN HE D

6. MOLINELLI, STEVE
   A MOLINAR, RICARDO B MOLINER, LOUISA C MOLINI, OSCAR D

7. PARRILLA, EMANUEL
   A PARRAS, TONY B PARRETTA, JOSEPHINE C PARRETTA, NANCY D

8. SILBERFARD, MILDRED
   A SILBERBERG, SEYMOUR B SILBERBLATT, JOHN C SILBERFARB, SYLVIA D

9. TOLANI, ROHET
   A TOLAN, DOROTHY B TOLASSI, JOANNA C TOLBERT, ALICE D

10. VIERA, DIANE
    A VIERA, DIANA B VIERA, ELLIOT C VIERA, JAMES D

11. KLAUER, MICHAEL
    A KLAUBER, ALFRED B KLAUBERG, SUSAN C KLAUS, MARJORIE D

12. REEVES, MARIE
    A REEVES, MATTHEW B REEVES, MELVIN C REEVES, ORALEE D

13. DEL VALLE, JULIA
    A DEL VALLE, EMMA B DEL VALLE, GLORIA C DEL VALLE, JOSEPH D

14. LAIO, SHU-YU
    A LAING, VINCENT B LAIRO, SCOTT C LAIS, STEVE D

15. MENDEZ, ROBERTO
    A MENDELSON, SOL B MENDES, MAE C MENDOZA, HUGO D

2 (#4)

16. ALBRIGHT, LEE 16.____
    A ALBRACHT, MARIE B ALBRECHT, VICTOR C ALBRINK, JOAN D

17. CAIN, STEPHEN 17.____
    A CAIN, SAMUEL B CAIN, SHARON C CAIN, SIBOL D

18. HOPKOWITZ, THOMAS 18.____
    A HOPKINS, CYNTHIA B HOPPENFELD, DENIS C HOPPER, ELSA D

19. LUMBLY, KAREN 19.____
    A LUMBI, JENNY B LUME, JIMMIE C LUMEN, GAIL D

20. MAYER, MORTON 20.____
    A MAYER, MONROE B MAYER, MORRIS C MAYER, MYRON D

21. YOUNGER, LORRAINE 21.____
    A YOUNGHEM, THEODORE B YOUNGMAN, LEIF C YOUNGS, FRED D

22. THORSEN, HILDA 22.____
    A THORNWELL, PERCY B THORON, LLOYD C THORP, JACQUELINE D

23. MC DERMOTT, BETTY 23.____
    A MC DEARMON, WILLIAM B MC DEVITT, BERYL C MC DONAGH, DANIEL D

24. BLUMENTHAL, SIMON 24.____
    A BLUMENTHAL, SHIRLEY B BLUMENTHAL, SIDNEY C BLUMENTHAL, SOLOMON D

25. ERVINS, RICHARD 25.____
    A ERVIN, BERTHA B ERVING, THELMA C ERWIN, EUGENE D

KEY (CORRECT ANSWERS)

1.	B	11.	C
2.	D	12.	A
3.	D	13.	D
4.	C	14.	B
5.	A	15.	C
6.	B	16.	C
7.	D	17.	D
8.	D	18.	B
9.	B	19.	B
10.	B	20.	C

21. A
22. D
23. B
24. C
25. C

TEST 5

DIRECTIONS: For each of the following, you are given a name above and three other names in alphabetical order below. The letters A, B, C, and D stand for spaces where you could file the name. Find the CORRECT space for the name given above so that it will be in alphabetical order with the names below it. The letter that stands for that space is the answer to the question.

1. GUIDRY, THELMA
   A GUIDONE, GEORGE B GUIGLI, PAMELA C GUIGNON, DANIEL D
   1._____

2. JAMES, ALLAN
   A JAMES, ALMA B JAMES, AMY C JAMES, ANNA D
   2._____

3. LESSOFF, CONNIE
   A LESSIK, JAKE B LESSING, LEONARD C LESSNER, ADELE D
   3._____

4. MONTNER, LUIS
   A MONTEFIORE, ANDREW B MONTILLA, IRIS C MONTINI, ALEXANDRA D
   4._____

5. PHELPS, KENNETH
   A PHELEN, JAMES B PHELON, RANDY C PHETT, GARY D
   5._____

6. STAVSKY, STANLEY
   A STAVROS, MIKE B STAWSKI, LILLIAN C STAWSKI, NAOMI D
   6._____

7. GROSSMAN, WILL
   A GROSSMAN, WENDY B GROSSMANN, WAYNE C GROSSMANN, WILLA D
   7._____

8. IRES, JEFFREY
   A IRENA, THOMAS B IRENE, JAY C IRES, HOWARD D
   8._____

9. NIKOLAOU, CHRISTINE
   A NIKOLAIS, GERRARD B NIKOLAKAKOS, GEORGE C NIKOLATOS, HARRY D
   9._____

10. TURCO, KEITH
    A TURCHIN, DEBORAH B TURCI, GINA C TURCK, KATHRYN D
    10._____

11. WORLEY, DIANE
    A WORMAN, STELLA B WORMER, SARA C WORMLEY, ROBERT D
    11._____

12. DRUSIN, GUY
    A DRURY, JESSICA B DRUSE, KEN C DRUSS, THERESA D
    12._____

13. LYONS, JAMES
    A LYONS, ERNST B LYONS, INGRID C LYONS, KEVIN D
    13._____

14. NOBLE, BERNARD
    A NOBEL, LOUISE B NOBILE, DENNIS C NOBIS, JAMES D
    14._____

15. O'DELL, ERIN
    A O'DAY, PATRICIA B O'DEA, MAUREEN C O'DELL, GWYNN D
    15._____

16. POUPON, LOUIS
    A POULSON, SIMON B POURE, DAMIAN C POURIDAS, CARMEN D

    16.____

17. REMEY, NAOMI
    A REMES, STUART B REMEZ, ALFREDO C REMIEN, ROBERT D

    17.____

18. WATSON, LAURENCE
    A WATSON, LENORA B WATSON, LEONARD C WATSON, LLOYD D

    18.____

19. AMSILI, MORTON
    A AMSDEN, ESTHER B AMSEL, HYMAN C ARES, MEYER D

    19.____

20. CLEMMONS, BERTHA
    A CLEMENT, GILBERT B CLEMINSON, DEAN C CLEMONS, GLADYS D

    20.____

21. LAMPERT, EDNA
    A LAMPIER, JANICE B LAMPKIN, ALYCE C LAMPKOWSKI, DENNIS D

    21.____

22. LIBERTO, DON
    A LIBERMAN, MATTIE B LIBERSON, MIRIAM C LIBERTY, ARTHUR D

    22.____

23. REVENZON, ISABELLA
    A REVELEY, RUTH B REVELLE, GRACE C REVERE, EDITH D

    23.____

24. BURKHALTER, HAZEL
    A BURKE, WINSTON B BURKETT, BENJAMIN C BURKEY, WAYNE D

    24.____

25. DORSEY, HAROLD
    A DOSHER, EILEEN B DOSHIRE, BURTON C DOSSIL, RICHARD D

    25.____

KEY (CORRECT ANSWERS)

1.	B	11.	A
2.	A	12.	C
3.	D	13.	C
4.	D	14.	D
5.	C	15.	C
6.	B	16.	B
7.	B	17.	B
8.	D	18.	A
9.	C	19.	C
10.	D	20.	C

21. A
22. C
23. C
24. D
25. A

TEST 6

DIRECTIONS: For each of the following, you are given a name above and three other names in alphabetical order below. The letters A, B, C, and D stand for spaces where you could file the name. Find the CORRECT space for the name given above so that it will be in alphabetical order with the names below it. The letter that stands for that space is the answer to the question.

1. HATFIELD, NICOLA
   A HATCHER, JOHN B HATELY, BRIAN C HATGIS, ELLEN D

   1.____

2. IVANOFF, HELENA
   A IVAN, LEONARD B IVANOV, SERGE C IVANY, EMERY D

   2.____

3. KELKER, NORMAN
   A KELFER, STEPHANE B KELING, JAY C KELISON, ABE D

   3.____

4. ROGGENBURG, LEE
   A ROGERS, SHARON B ROGET, ALLAN C ROGGERO, MORGAN D

   4.____

5. SMITH, ALENA
   A SMITH, AARON B SMITH, AGNES C SMITH, ALBERT D

   5.____

6. ZOLOR, RONALD
   A ZOLNAK, SUSANNA B ZOLOTH, SAMUEL C ZOLOTO, PEARL D

   6.____

7. ERRICH, GRETCHEN
   A ERREICH, RENE B ERRERA, STEVEN C ERRETT, ALICE D

   7.____

8. CARDWELL, MELASAN
   A CARDUCCI, RONALD B CARDULLO, MIKE C CARDY, FREDRIK D

   8.____

9. MOFFAT, SARAH
   A MOFFET, JONATHAN B MOFFIE, LISA C MOFFITT, LAUREN D

   9.____

10. PARRINO, WAYNE
    A PARRETTA, MICHELE B PARRILLA, BERNIE C PARRINELLO, CARRIE D

    10.____

11. PINSLEY, SETH
    A PINSKY, GLORIA B PINSON, BENNET C PINTADO, MARIE D

    11.____

12. FREEMAN, ELMIRA
    A FREEMAN, EDITH B FREEMAN, ERIC C FREEMAN, ETHEL D

    12.____

13. BERLINGER, SOPHIE
    A BERLEY, DAVID B BERLIND, ARNOLD C BERLINGER, FREDA D

    13.____

14. ANIELLO, JOSEPH
    A ANGULO, ADOLFO B ANHALT, LINDA C ANIBAL, VINCENT D

    14.____

15. LACHER, LEO
    A LACHET, MARGARET B LACHINI, KAY C LACHIVER, ANDREA D

    15.____

16. ROBINSON, MARION
    A ROBINSON, MARCIA B ROBINSON, MARGARET C ROBINSON, MARIETTA D

    16.____

17. ULRICH, DENNIS
    A ULMAN, CANDY B ULMER, TED C ULRIED, RICHARD D

    17.____

18. ASHINSKY, ROSS
    A ASHKAR, MICHAEL B ASHKE, PAUL C ASHKIN, ROBERTA D

    18.____

19. LITVAK, DARRELL
    A LITUCHY, BEVERLY B LITVIN, SAM C LITWACK, MARTIN D

    19.____

20. SLATTERY, GERALD
    A SLATER, NELLIE B SLATKIN, HEIDI C SLATKY, IRVING D

    20.____

21. MCCANTS, GEORGIA
    A MCCANN, CHERYL B MCCANNA, THOMAS C MCCARDELL, GARY D

    21.____

22. HARMER, AVA
    A HARLOW, JULES B HARLSON, NORMAN C HARMEL, SHARON D

    22.____

23. CALDERONE, PHILIP
    A CALDERIN, ANA B CALDON, WALTER C CALDRON, MICHELE D

    23.____

24. GINSBURG, ISAAC
    A GINSBURG, EDWARD B GINSBURG, GERALD C GINSBURG, HILDA D

    24.____

25. LEE, LEIGH
    A LEE, LELA B LEE, LELAND C LEE, LEON D

    25.____

KEY (CORRECT ANSWERS)

1.	C	11.	B
2.	B	12.	B
3.	D	13.	D
4.	C	14.	D
5.	D	15.	A
6.	B	16.	D
7.	D	17.	C
8.	C	18.	A
9.	A	19.	B
10.	D	20.	D

21. C
22. D
23. B
24. D
25. A

TEST 7

DIRECTIONS: For each of the following, you are given a name above and three other names in alphabetical order below. The letters A, B, C, and D stand for spaces where you could file the name. Find the CORRECT space for the name given above so that it will be in alphabetical order with the names below it. The letter that stands for that space is the answer to the question.

1. POWERS, PHYLLIS
   A POWELL, HATTIE B POWER, EDWARD C POWLETT, WENDY D   1._____

2. SILVERA, IRWIN
   A SILVA, ANGEL B SILVANO, FRANK C SILVERIA, ANNA D   2._____

3. BACHRACH, DAN
   A BACHMANN, DONNA B BACHNER, LESTER C BACHOWSKI, JEWEL D   3._____

4. RIVERA, RAMON
   A RIVAS, ERICA B RIVES, SHARON C RIVIER, CLAUDE D   4._____

5. WEINSTOCK, JEFFREY
   A WEINSTEIN, PAUL B WEINSTONE, ALAN C WEINTRAUB, MARCI D   5._____

6. AMANDA, STEPHAN
   A AMADO, DANIELLO B AMALIA, JOSE C AMAR, LISA D   6._____

7. HERRON, LOUIS
   A HERSCH, JACK B HERSCHELL, GREGORY C HERSCHER, GAIL D   7._____

8. REEDY, ARTHUR
   A REED, ALEX B REESE, JOHN C REEVE, DAVE D   8._____

9. FLORIN, RAYMOND
   A FLORENTINO, PAULA B FLORES, MITCHEL C FLORIAN, CARLO D   9._____

10. HOROWITZ, ELLIOT
    A HOROWITZ, FRANKLIN B HOROWITZ, IRA C HOROWITZ, JOAN D   10._____

11. KNOPFLER, WOODY
    A KNOBLER, HENRY B KNOLL, GEORGE C KNOPF, LAURA D   11._____

12. OTIN, JENNIFER
    A OTERO, ALBERT B OTHON, DOROTHY C OTIS, JAMES D   12._____

13. SACHA, IRENE
    A SACCO, HEATHER B SACHNER, JULIE C SACHS, DAVID D   13._____

14. WORTHY, PRISCILLA
    A WORTH, ROBERT B WORTHINGTON, SUSAN C WORTMAN, MYRA D   14._____

15. ZUCKERMAN, GARY
    A ZUKER, JEROME B ZUKOWSKI, CHRIS C ZULACK, JOHN D   15._____

2 (#7)

16. BRIEGER, CLARENCE 16. ____
   A BRIEF, SIGMUND B BRIELLE, JEAN C BRIELOFF, SAUL D

17. FOSTER, AGNES 17. ____
   A FOSTER, ADDIE B FOSTER, ALBERT C FOSTER, ALICE D

18. LIBERSTEIN, MIRIAM 18. ____
   A LIBERMAN, HERMAN B LIBERSON, RUBIN C LIBERT, NAT D

19. PRICKETT, DELORES 19. ____
   A PRICE, WILLIAM B PRICHARD, STEPHANY C PRITCHETT, KENNETH D

20. TRIBBLE, RITA 20. ____
   A TRIAS, JOSE B TRIBBIT, CHARLES C TRIBE, SIENNA D

21. ZOBEL, MAX 21. ____
   A ZOBACK, DERRICK B ZOBALI, KIERSTAN C ZOBERG, STUART D

22. HOTRA, WALTER 22. ____
   A HOTT, NELL B HOTTENSEN, ROBERT C HOTTON, BRUCE D

23. MICHELL, CARL 23. ____
   A MICHELE, KAREN B MICHELMAN, BERTHA C MICHELS, GLORIA D

24. RAFFERTY, GEORGE 24. ____
   A RAFFERTY, HAROLD B RAFFERTY, KEVIN C RAFFERTY, LUCILLE D

25. OLIVIERI, ALLAN 25. ____
   A OLIVIERO, FRANK B OLIVRY, RAUL C OLIZEIRA, CHARLES D

KEY (CORRECT ANSWERS)

1. C
2. C
3. D
4. B
5. B

6. C
7. A
8. B
9. D
10. A

11. D
12. C
13. B
14. C
15. A

16. B
17. B
18. C
19. C
20. C

21. C
22. A
23. B
24. A
25. A

ARITHMETICAL COMPUTATION AND REASONING
EXAMINATION SECTION
TEST 1

DIRECTIONS: Each question or incomplete statement is followed by several suggested answers or completions. Select the one that BEST answers the question or completes the statement. *PRINT THE LETTER OF THE CORRECT ANSWER IN THE SPACE AT THE RIGHT.*

1. 3/8 less than $40 is
   A. $25   B. $65   C. $15   D. $55

2. 27/64 expressed as a percent is
   A. 40.625%   B. 42.188%   C. 43.750%   D. 45.313%

3. 1/6 more than 36 gross is _____ gross.
   A. 6   B. 48   C. 30   D. 42

4. 15 is 20% of

5. The number which when increased by 1/3 of itself equals 96 is
   A. 128   B. 72   C. 64   D. 32

6. 0.16 3/4 written as percent is
   A. 16 3/4%   B. 16.3/4%   C. .016 3/4%   D. .0016 3/4%

7. 55% of 15 is
   A. 82.5   B. 0.825   C. 0.0825   D. 8.25

8. The number which when decreased by 1/3 of itself equals 96 is
   A. 64   B. 32   C. 128   D. 144

9. A carpenter used a board 15 3/4 ft. long from which 3 footstools were made with sufficient lumber left over for half of another footstool.
   If the lumber cost 24 1/2¢ per foot, the cost of EACH footstool was
   A. $1.54   B. $3.86   C. $1.10   D. $1.08

10. In one year, a luncheonette purchased 1231 gallons of milk for $907.99.
    The AVERAGE cost per half pint was
    A. $0.046   B. $0.045   C. $0.047   D. $0.044

11. The product of 23 and 9 3/4 is
    A. 191 2/3   B. 224 1/4   C. 213 3/4   D. 32 3/4

12. An order for 345 machine bolts at $4.15 per hundred will cost
    A. $0.1432   B. $1.1432   C. $14.32   D. $143.20

13. The fractional equivalent of .0625 is 13.____
   A. 1/16   B. 1/15   C. 1/14   D. 1/13

14. The number 0.03125 equals 14.____
   A. 3/64   B. 1/16   C. 1/64   D. 1/32

15. 21.70 divided by 1.75 equals 15.____
   A. 124   B. 12.4   C. 1.24   D. .124

16. The average cost of school lunches for 100 children varied as follows: Monday, $0.285; Tuesday, $0.237; Wednesday, $0.264; Thursday, $0.276; Friday, $0.292. The AVERAGE lunch cost 16.____
   A. $0.136   B. $0.270   C. $0.135   D. $0.271

17. The cost of 5 dozen eggs at $8.52 per gross is 17.____
   A. $3.50   B. $42.60   C. $3.55   D. $3.74

18. 410.07 less 38.49 equals 18.____
   A. 372.58   B. 371.58   C. 381.58   D. 382.68

19. The cost of 7 3/4 tons of coal at $20.16 per ton is 19.____
   A. $15.12   B. $151.20   C. $141.12   D. $156.24

20. The sum of 90.79, 79.09, 97.90, and 9.97 is 20.____
   A. 277.75   B. 278.56   C. 276.94   D. 277.93

KEY (CORRECT ANSWERS)

1.	A	11.	B
2.	B	12.	C
3.	D	13.	A
4.	C	14.	D
5.	B	15.	B
6.	A	16.	D
7.	D	17.	C
8.	D	18.	B
9.	C	19.	D
10.	A	20.	A

3 (#1)

SOLUTIONS TO PROBLEMS

1. ($40)(5/8) = $25

2. 27/64 = .421875 ≈ 42.188%

3. (36)(1 1/6) = 42

4. Let x = missing number. Then, 15 = .20x. Solving, x = 75

5. Let x = missing number. Then, x + 1/3 x = 96. Simplifying, 4/3 x = 96. Solving, x = 96 ÷ 4/3 = 72

6. .16 3/4 = 16 3/4% by simply moving the decimal point two places to the right.

7. (.55)(15) = 8.25

8. Let x = missing number. Then, x - 1/3 x = 96. Simplifying, 2/3 x = 96. Solving, x = 96 ÷ 2/3 = 144

9. 15 3/4 ÷ 3 1/2 = 4.5 feet per footstool. The cost of one footstool is ($.245)(4.5) = $1.1025 ≈ $1.10

10. $907.99 ÷ 1231 = $.7376 per gallon. Since there are 16 half-pints in a gallon, the average cost per half-pint is $.7376 ÷ 16 ≈ $.046

11. (23)(9 3/4) = (23)(9.75) = 224.25 or 224 1/4

12. ($4.15)(3.45) = $14.3175 = $14.32

13. .0625 = 625/10,000 = 1/16

14. .03125 = 3125/100,000 = 1/32

15. 21.70 ÷ 1.75 = 12.4

16. The sum of these lunches is $1.354. Then, $1.354 ÷ 5 = $.2708 = $.271

17. $8.52 ÷ 12 = $.71 per dozen. Then, the cost of 5 dozen is ($.71)(5) = $3.55

18. 410.07 - 38.49 = 371.58

19. ($20.16)(7.75) = $156.24

20. 90.79 + 79.09 + 97.90 + 9.97 = 277.75

TEST 2

DIRECTIONS: Each question or incomplete statement is followed by several suggested answers or completions. Select the one that BEST answers the question or completes the statement. *PRINT THE LETTER OF THE CORRECT ANSWER IN THE SPACE AT THE RIGHT.*

1. 1600 is 40% of what number?
   A. 6400 B. 3200 C. 4000 D. 5600

2. An executive's time card reads: Arrived 9:15 A.M., Left 2:05 P.M. How many hours was he in the office? _____ hours _____ minutes.
   A. 5; 10 B. 4; 50 C. 4; 10 D. 5; 50

3. .4266 times .3333 will have the following number of decimals in the product:
   A. 8 B. 4 C. 1 D. None of these

4. An office floor is 25 ft. wide by 36 ft. long. To cover this floor with carpet will require _____ square yards.
   A. 100 B. 300 C. 900 D. 25

5. 1/8 of 1% expressed as a decimal is
   A. .125 B. .0125 C. 1.25 D. .00125

6. $\dfrac{6 \div 4}{6 \times 4}$ equals 6x4
   A. 1/16 B. 1 C. 1/6 D. 1/4

7. 1/25 of 230 equals
   A. 92.0 B. 9.20 C. .920 D. 920

8. 4 times 3/8 equals
   A. 1 3/8 B. 3/32 C. 12.125 D. 1.5

9. 3/4 divided by 4 equals
   A. 3 B. 3/16 C. 16/3 D. 16

10. 6/7 divided by 2/7 equals
    A. 6 B. 12/49 C. 3 D. 21

11. The interest on $240 for 90 days ' 6% is
    A. $4.80 B. $3.40 C. $4.20 D. $3.60

12. 16 2/3% of 1728 is
    A. 91 B. 288 C. 282 D. 280

13. 6 1/4% of 6400 is   13._____
    A. 2500   B. 410   C. 108   D. 400

14. 12 1/2% of 560 is   14._____
    A. 65   B. 40   C. 50   D. 70

15. 2 yards divided by 3 equals   15._____
    A. 2 feet   B. 1/2 yard   C. 3 yards   D. 3 feet

16. A school has 540 pupils. 45% are boys. How many girls are there in this school?   16._____
    A. 243   B. 297   C. 493   D. 394

17. .1875 is equivalent to   17._____
    A. 18 3/4   B. 75/18   C. 18/75   D. 3/16

18. A kitchen cabinet listed at $42 is sold for $33.60. The discount allowed is   18._____
    A. 10%   B. 15%   C. 20%   D. 30%

19. 3 6/8 divided by 8 1/4 equals   19._____
    A. 9 1/8   B. 12   C. 5/11   D. 243.16

20. An agent sold goods to the amount of $1480. His commission at 5 1/2% was   20._____
    A. $37.50   B. $81.40   C. 76.70   D. $81.10

KEY (CORRECT ANSWERS

1. C   11. D
2. B   12. B
3. A   13. D
4. A   14. D
5. D   15. A

6. A   16. B
7. B   17. D
8. D   18. C
9. B   19. C
10. C   20. B

3 (#2)

SOLUTIONS TO PROBLEMS

1. Let x = missing number. Then, 1600 = .40x. Solving, x = 4000

2. 2:05 PM - 9:15 AM = 4 hours 50 minutes

3. The product of two 4-decimal numbers is an 8-decimal number.

4. (25 ft)(36 ft) = 900 sq.ft. = 100 sq.yds.

5. (1/8)(1%) = (.125)(.01) = .00125

6. (6 ÷ 4) ÷ (6 x 4) = 3/2 ÷ 24 = (3/2)(1/24) = (1/16)

7. (1/25)(230) = 9.20

8. (4)(3/8) = 12/8 = 1.5

9. 3/4 ÷ 4 = (3/4)(1/4) = 3/16

10. 6/7 / 2/7 = (6/7)(7/2) = 3

11. ($240)(.06)(90/360) = $3.60

12. (16 2/3%)(1728) = (1/6)(1728) = 288

13. (6 1/4%)(6400) = (1/16)(6400) = 400

14. (12 1/2%)(560) = (1/8)(560) = 70

15. 2 yds ÷ 3 = 2/3 yds = (2/3)(3) = 2 ft.

16. If 45% are boys, then 55% are girls. Thus, (540)(.55) = 297

17. .1875 = 1875/10,000 = 3/16

18. $42 - $33.60 = $8.40.
    The discount is $8.40 ÷ $42 = .20 = 20%

19. 3 6/8 - 8 1/4 = (30/8)(4/33) = 5/11

20. ($1480)(.055) = $81.40

TEST 3

DIRECTIONS: Each question or incomplete statement is followed by several suggested answers or completions. Select the one that BEST answers the question or completes the statement. *PRINT THE LETTER OF THE CORRECT ANSWER IN THE SPACE AT THE RIGHT.*

1. 93.648 divided by 0.4 is
   A. 23.412   B. 234.12   C. 2.3412   D. 2341.2

2. Add 4.3682, .0028, 34., 9.92, and from the sum subtract 1.992. The remainder is
   A. .46299   B. 4.6299   C. 462.99   D. 46.299

3. At $2.88 per gross, three dozen will cost
   A. $8.64   B. $0.96   C. $0.72   D. $11.52

4. 13 times 2.39 times 0.024 equals
   A. 745.68   B. 74.568   C. 7.4568   D. .74568

5. A living room suite is marked $64 less 25 percent. A cash discount of 10 percent is allowed. The cash price is
   A. $53.20   B. $47.80   C. $36.00   D. $43.20

6. 1/8 of 1 percent expressed as a decimal is
   A. .125   B. .0125   C. 1.25   D. .00125

7. 16 percent of 482.11 equals
   A. 77.1376   B. 771.4240   C. 7714.2400   D. 7.71424

8. A merchant sold a chair for $60. This was at a profit of 25 percent of what it cost him. The chair cost him
   A. $48   B. $45   C. $15   D. $75

9. Add 5 hours 13 minutes, 3 hours 49 minutes, and 14 minutes. The sum is _____ hours _____ minutes.
   A. 9; 16   B. 9;76   C. 8;16   D. 8;6

10. 89 percent of $482 is
    A. $428.98   B. $472.36   C. $42.90   D. $47.24

11. 200 percent of 800 is
    A. 16   B. 1600   C. 2500   D. 4

12. Add 2 feet 3 inches, 4 feet 11 inches, 8 inches, 6 feet 6 inches. The sum is _____ feet _____ inches.
    A. 12; 4   B. 12; 14   C. 14; 4   D. 14; 28

13. A merchant bought dresses at $15 each and sold them at $20 each. His overhead   13.____
    expenses are 20 percent of cost. His net profit on each dress is

    A. $1   B. $2   C. $3   D. $4

14. 0.0325 expressed as a percent is   14.____

    A. 325%   B. 3 1/4%   C. 32 1/2%   D. 32.5%

15. Add 3/4, 1/8, 1/32, 1/2; and from the sum subtract 4/8. The remainder is   15.____

    A. 2/32   B. 7/8   C. 29/32   D. 3/4

16. A salesman gets a commission of 4 percent on his sales. If he wants his commission to   16.____
    amount to $40, he will have to sell merchandise totaling

    A. $160   B. $10   C. $1,000   D. $100

17. Jones borrowed $225,000 for five years at 3 1/2 percent. The annual interest charge   17.____
    was

    A. $1,575   B. $1,555   C. $7,875   D. $39,375

18. A kitchen cabinet listed at $42 is sold for $33.60. The discount allowed is _____ per-   18.____
    cent.

    A. 10   B. 15   C. 20   D. 30

19. The exact number of days from May 5, 2007 to July 1, 2007 is _____ days.   19.____

    A. 59   B. 58   C. 56   D. 57

20. A dealer sells an article at a loss of 50% of the cost. Based on the selling price, the loss   20.____
    is

    A. 25%   B. 50%   C. 100%   D. none of these

KEY (CORRECT ANSWERS)

1.	B	11.	B
2.	D	12.	C
3.	C	13.	B
4.	D	14.	B
5.	D	15.	C
6.	D	16.	C
7.	A	17.	C
8.	A	18.	C
9.	A	19.	D
10.	A	20.	C

SOLUTIONS TO PROBLEMS

1. $93.648 \div .4 = 234.12$

2. $4.368 + .0028 + 34 + 9.92 - 1.992 = 48.291 - 1.992 = 46.299$

3. $2.88 for 12 dozen means $.24 per dozen. Three dozen will cost (3)($.24) = $.72

4. $(13)(2.39)(.024) = .74568$

5. $($64)(.75)(.90) = 43.20

6. $(1/8)(1\%) = (.125)(.01) = .00125$

7. $(.16)(482.11) = 77.1376$

8. Let x = cost. Then, $1.25x = 60. Solving, $x = 48

9. 5 hrs. 13 min. + 3 hrs. 49 min. + 14 min = 8 hrs. 76 min.

10. $(.89)($482) = 428.98

11. $200\% = 2$. So, $(200\%)(800) = (2)(800) = 1600$

12. 2 ft. 3 in. + 4 ft. 11 in. + 8 in. + 6 ft. 6 in. + 12 ft. 28 in. = 14 ft. 4 in.

13. Overhead is $(.20)($15) = 3. The net profit is $20 - $15 - $3 = $2

14. $.0325 = 3.25\% = 3\ 1/4\%$

15. $3/4 + 1/8 + 1/32 + 1/2 - 4/8 = 45/32 - 4/8 = 29/32$

16. Let x = sales. Then, $$40 = .04x$. Solving, $x = 1000

17. Annual interest is $($225,000)(.035) \times 1 = 7875$

18. $42 - $33.60 = 8.40. Then, $$8.40 \div $42 = .20 = 20\%$

19. The number of days left for May, June, July is 26, 30, and 1. Thus, $26 + 30 + 1 = 57$

20. Let x = cost, so that $.50x$ = selling price. The loss is represented by $.50x \div .50x = 1 = 100\%$ on the selling price. (Note: The loss in dollars is $x - .50x = .50x$)

GUIDELINES FOR EFFECTIVE TELEPHONE COMMUNICATIONS

"Telephone" come from a Greek word, which means "to speak at a distance."

Business and non-business calls combined, billions of telephone calls are completed on an average day throughout the year.

Telephone selling is more personal and more direct than selling through the mail.

The telephone may be used in telephone marketing for 1) order solicitation, 2) to set up sales appointments, 3) lead generation, 4) renewals (calls to present customers for repeat business), 5) marginal account coverage (to contact client accounts whose volume is too small.

The following suggestions are offered to the general public, telephone operators, office personnel salesmen, and executives.

1. BE FRIENDLY—Some busy executives release their daily tensions on the telephone. They become impatient, irritated and even hostile.
   The effective communicator maintains a positive mental attitude when speaking on the phone.
2. IMPROVE YOUR VOICE RANGE—A lowered voice sounds warmer and friendlier than a high pitched voice. If you tend to use a high pitched voice, you can take a pen or pencil in your hand and practice lowering your voice as you lower the object in your hand. Repeating this exercise while speaking on the phone will improve your speaking voice range.
3. GESTURE WHILE YOU SPEAK—Gestures are a part of human behavior that even computerized robots cannot duplicate. Gestures are a natural part of speaking behavior.
   Using gestures while you speak on the telephone will make your telephone voice more natural.
   Smile into the telephone-express yourself, show enthusiasm, get excited, and be sincere.
4. SAY WHAT YOU MEAN—People can't see your expression when you talk on the phone, so say what you want to express.
5. LISTEN CAREFULLY—If you do not listen carefully to what the other person is saying, you can't be sure that you're carrying on effective communication. Listen carefully so that the person you are speaking with does not say..."I know you believe you understand what you think I said. But I'm not sure you realize that what you heard is not what I meant."
6. BE COURTEOUS—You are more likely to get cooperation if you make your requests politely.
7. SIMPLIFY YOUR MESSAGE—Make separate calls for different purposes. If you have to make separate points, state them clearly by using numerical identification. For example, point one, point two and point three.
8. STRUCTURE YOUR CONVERSATION—Think about the purpose of different types of calls and how you can structure them so that you can communicate most effectively. The more effectively you communicate on the phone, the more time you save.
9. EXPRESS YOURSELF CLEARLY—In seeking to give style and effectiveness to the wording and phrasing of a speech, one must never forget that clearness of expression is the first imperative. Everything in style must yield to clarity.

10. PACE YOUR CONVERSATION – Don't speak too slowly, otherwise you will bore your listener.
People are more attentive when you speak at a quick pace, provided that you are not speaking so fast that others cannot understand what you are saying.

www.ingramcontent.com/pod-product-compliance
Lightning Source LLC
Chambersburg PA
CBHW082122230426
43671CB00015B/2781